VINYL ME, PLEASE

VINYL ME, PLEASE

100 Albums You Need in Your Collection

Abrams Image | New York

CONTENTS

VINYL ME,
PLEASE

ARTIST
The War On Drugs

TITLE
LOST IN THE DREAM

EDITION
AUG / 2014

PACKAGED

CONTRIBUTORS

Tyler Barstow is the co-founder of Vinyl Me, Please and their head of content. He's a bargain-bin Matt Berninger and likes listening to people talk about space. He hopes one day to be a quarter of the writer Lorrie Moore is.

Donivan Berube quit his job in 2013 and put his apartment into storage to travel and live out of a tent. He makes music as Blessed Feathers.

Tom Breihan is the senior editor at *Stereogum*, and he's written for *Grantland*, *GQ*, *Slate*, *The A.V. Club*, *Pitchfork*, and the *Village Voice*, among others. He lives in Charlottesville, Virginia.

Matthew Davis (MD) is the label manager of Flying Nun Records, as well as the chairman of Independent Music New Zealand (IMNZ). He was instrumental in the label's rejuvenation in 2011. A keen indoor-cricket player, Matthew retired from the Mt Vic Division-3 team with a strike rate of 109 and an average of 41.

Michael Depland is the music editor at *UPROXX*. He resides in New York City, but only until Texas calls him back home. He can easily be bribed with the promise of breakfast tacos or fresh biscuits.

Tyler Hayes is obsessed with technology and music, both individually and how they intertwine. He has written extensively for *Fast Company*, *Paste*, and lots of other publications about the two industries.

Chris Lay is a freelance writer, archivist, and record-store clerk living in Madison, Wisconsin. The first CD he bought for himself was the *Dumb and Dumber* soundtrack when he was 12, and things only got better from there.

Andrew Martin is a freelance music writer (and full-time content marketing manager) residing in Raleigh, North Carolina. He spends his free time building his jazz and hip-hop vinyl collection, slogging through his videogame queue, and hanging out with his wife and their two cats.

Drew Millard is a writer/editor/journalist/ critic/blogger living in Los Angeles. He owns one (1) dog, one (1) hoverboard, and just three (3) screw tapes.

Ben Munson is a full-time editor, freelance writer, and former city editor for *The A.V. Club Madison*. He prefers '90s R&B when he's cooking and dreams of the day he'll be able to hand down his Beatnuts records to his daughter.

Andy O'Connor's mom bought him a copy of *Fargo Rock City* during his freshman year of high school, hoping he would become the next Klosterman and bring honor to the O'Connor name. Instead, he's a metal critic who lives in Austin, Texas. At least he's the best metal critic living in Austin.

Michael Penn II (rap name CRASHprez) is a 22-year-old hip-hop artist, journalist, facilitator, and curator from a suburb of black folks called Fort Washington, Maryland. He spent his four undergrad years in Wisconsin— through the First Wave scholarship—searching for the perfect chicken spot and learning to turn shit up on the page and on the stage.

Geoff Rickly is the former and current singer of bands Thursday, United Nations, Ink & Dagger, and No Devotion. He's a bass player in NARX, a producer of My Chemical Romance, and a music lover.

Sarah Sahim is a UK-based freelance pop culture writer. Her work has previously appeared in *Rolling Stone*, *Pitchfork*, the *Guardian*, and others.

Cameron Schaefer is head of music and label relations for Vinyl Me, Please. A former Air Force pilot, he now lives in Louisville, Colorado, with his wife, three children, and records.

Levi J Sheppard and **Joshua Lingenfelter** grew up listening to music together from a very early age—playing pony-league baseball and hustling Columbia House record club using fake names for countless introductory offers. These days they still talk music nearly every day; Josh plays Aphex Twin as background music in the Advanced Placement Literature class he teaches, and Levi moonlights as a pilot in the Royal Air Force when he's not hanging around Vinyl Me, Please headquarters.

Jes Skolnik is the managing editor at Bandcamp and has regularly contributed writing to publications like *Pitchfork*, *Flavorwire*, and *Paper*. One of many, many people to have had their life fundamentally altered by punk, Jes plays in the band Split Feet and works on making DIY art spaces better places to be for everyone.

Gary Suarez is a music and culture writer, born, raised, and based in New York City. He has contributed to a variety of publications, including *Billboard*, *Complex*, *Forbes*, *Noisey*, *The Quietus*, and *Vulture*, among others.

Eric Sundermann is a writer based in Brooklyn, New York, who currently works as editor-in-chief of *Noisey*, VICE's music channel. Originally from Iowa, and a proud graduate of the University of Iowa, he's been writing about music—both for money and for free records—for nearly a decade, and his work has appeared in the *Village Voice*, *Rolling Stone*, *SPIN*, and more. One time, A$AP Rocky told him he has "British-guy swag."

Zach Swiecki is a graduate student living in Madison, Wisconsin. When he is not doing academic work, he is thinking about maybe trying to write something about music.

Caitlin White is a music and culture writer living in Brooklyn, New York. Her favorite Bob Dylan album is *Empire Burlesque*.

Andrew Winistorfer is assistant editor of content for Vinyl Me, Please, whose work has appeared in *Noisey*, *VICE*, *The A.V. Club*, *Guerilla Newspaper* (the underground newspaper he started in high school that almost got him suspended multiple times), and elsewhere. He lives in Madison, Wisconsin, with his girlfriend, their expanding collection of Ludacris and Nelly records, and their dog.

Luke Winkie is a writer and former pizza maker living in the hills of Los Angeles. You can read his work in *VICE*, *Rolling Stone*, *Gawker*, and everywhere else good content is found.

Susannah Young is a displaced Tennessean living in Chicago, Illinois, with her charming boyfriend (also a displaced Tennessean) and bossy rabbit, whose writing has appeared in *Pitchfork*, *Under the Radar*, and the *International Journal of Arts Management*, among other places. By day, she's a communications consultant to nonprofit organizations—which is an obtuse, corporate-speak way of describing her actual job: showing nonprofits how to talk about themselves in ways that make rich folks care about the specific ways said nonprofits propose saving the world.

INTRODUCTION

I want to believe we're living in a time when irony is being put out to pasture. So many of our most important words are regaining their single-entendre strength. I want to believe that phrases like "I love you," "it's beautiful," and "that was worth it" are beginning to be less of a barricade against loneliness and more of a rich, generous truth; less hungry-eyed insistence, and more good-hearted fact. I want to believe that because, while the Internet Age has been wonderful in many ways, it's been exhausting in many more. As the adage goes, for as much information as we have about the world around us now, we know less about ourselves and the ones we love. And it shows. It's harder to untangle ourselves from the myriad possible lives parading through our minds and commit to one in the real world. It feels scarier to put down roots.

As I was thinking about what would fit best as an introduction to this book, I was reminded of this quote from *The Writing Life*, Annie Dillard's essential handbook on exactly what you would guess. She wrote, "How we spend our days is, of course, how we spend our lives. What we do with this hour, and that one, is what we are doing." Simple, I know. All the most useful stuff is. And it burrows down to the heart of why we wrote this book. If our time and the way we spend it ends up being the essential piece of who we are, then what we listen to and the way we listen to it ends up being much more important than we may think. It means when we're talking about the music we love, we're talking about our life and our identity. It means that what's on our record shelves is serious stuff.

We started Vinyl Me, Please years ago with a simple idea: we all need to spend more time with albums that matter. Albums that are worth your time. And we've put together a list of one hundred records that we think are worth your focused attention. We aren't arguing that you have to like every single one of these, or that this is the only possible list like this that could be made. Instead, we humbly suggest that each of these records has something to teach you—from each individual track, to the carefully crafted album cover artworks, they all have something important to say. And as with all important things, it can take time to hear what that is. I'm not going to gripe about whether you're listening to these on a Crosley or a Pro-Ject or any other system. That's not what this book is for. What it's for, instead, is to give you a collection of works that each have a particular way of opening your eyes and introducing you to yourself; that each have something valuable to add to you. All one hundred of these bring with them their own stories, styles, characters, and lessons, and we've gathered some of the best writers we know to tell you all about them. I don't know where the process of listening all the way through this book will take you—it will be different for everyone—but I do know that in a tangible, unironic way, you will be better for it.

Tyler Barstow
Vinyl Me, Please co-founder, 2016

A-D

RYAN ADAMS
LIVE AT CARNEGIE HALL

by Luke Winkie

When all's said and done, Ryan Adams might have the most ridiculous career in the history of pop music. Rollicking Whiskeytown Ryan Adams; sad-boy derelict *Heartbreaker* Ryan Adams; Grammy-nominated, "New York, New York"–era *Gold* Ryan Adams; slightly infuriating "Wonderwall"-covering weirdo Ryan Adams; divergent, heavy-metal, are-we-sure-he's-okay Ryan Adams, and of course the equally divergent, Taylor Swift–covering, aren't-we-lucky-to-have-him Ryan Adams. He's released 15 albums, written two books, left one insane voicemail, and has worn out countless jean jackets. It's occasionally not been easy being a Ryan Adams fan, but it's certainly never been boring. I suppose that's all you can ask for.

On the other side of our last 15 years with Ryan Adams, we have a man who seems happy, artistically fulfilled, and big enough to play Carnegie Hall. The album cover artwork captures this neatly: Adams's rapt audience packing out the vast hall; the man himself hovering between the shadows and the spotlight. That's what you get on *Live at Carnegie Hall*: 42 tracks spanning two nights in the winter of 2014; just Ryan, his guitar, harmonica, and honeysuckle voice. Stripping everything down to an equal level, dodging his more polarizing work, and giving fans what they want. And you know what? Not a lot of people on earth can step to an opening triptych like "Oh My Sweet Carolina," "My Winding Wheel," and "Dirty Rain."

The vinyl release of *Live at Carnegie Hall* is particularly handsome—a box set spanning six 180-gram records, imbued with all the ultra-limited fetishistic qualities that make collecting a worthy hobby. And while it might not be the definitive Ryan Adams suite (like it or not, you *have* to include albums like *29* and *Orion* in the biography), it might be the Ryan Adams I enjoy the most. Calm, peaceful, and actually kind of funny. "I would assume many of you, probably like 86 percent of you, are on Paxil, so you understand about depression," he says during one particularly inspired bit of banter. "You're at a fucking Ryan Adams show, you know what I mean?"

Like this?
Check out these three too

Ryan Adams
Heartbreaker

Bob Dylan
Blood on the Tracks

Whiskeytown
Pneumonia

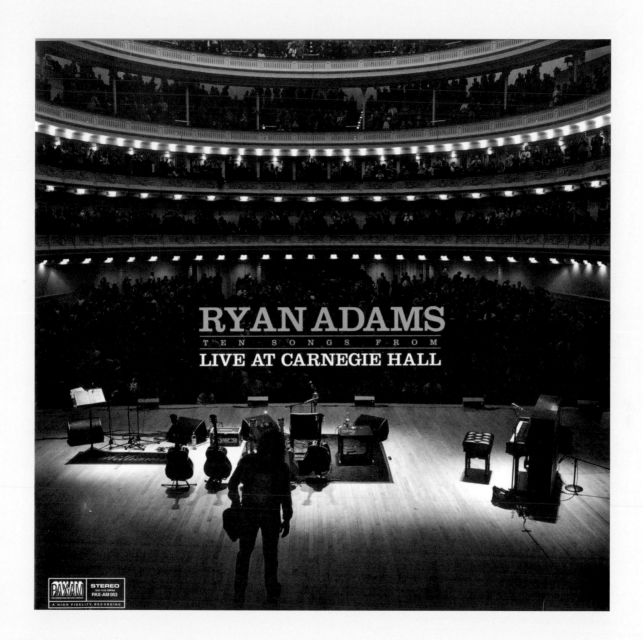

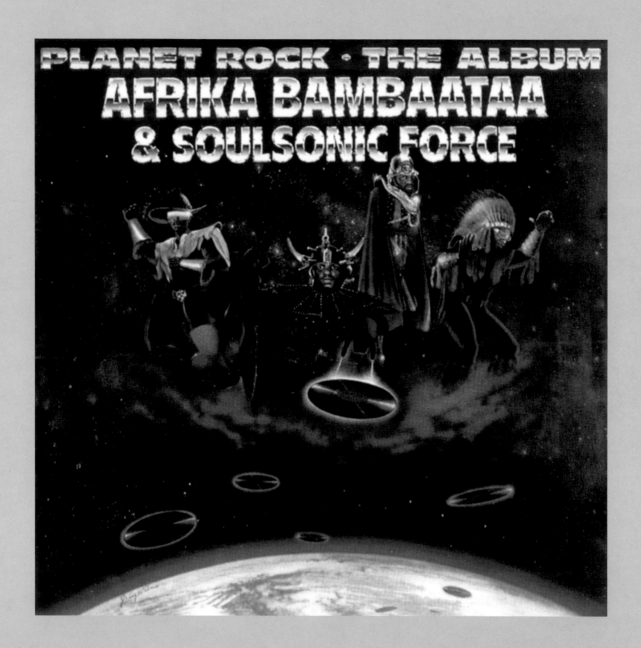

AFRIKA BAMBAATAA & SOULSONIC FORCE
PLANET ROCK: THE ALBUM

by Gary Suarez

Like so many members of hip-hop's first wave, Afrika Bambaataa came up during an era of gang factionalism and violent turf wars in New York City. A South Bronx native, he rose in the ranks of the Black Spades to become a warlord, a powerful title charged with some obvious responsibilities and duties. In the wake of 1971's historic Hoe Avenue Peace Meeting and that street summit's resultant treaty, Bambaataa built what would become a unifying, more peaceable organization ultimately dubbed the Universal Zulu Nation.

DJ Kool Herc's legendary parties brought everyone together regardless of affiliation, prompting the former warlord to pursue his own musical path (though the Afrofuturist artwork on the cover gives a nod to Bambaataa's warrior status). With co-production by dance-music pioneers Arthur Baker and John Robie, "Planet Rock" drew from Kraftwerk and Yellow Magic Orchestra to make something undeniably hip-hop, fusing two nascent genres in the process. A milestone in modern music history, the track was followed by the electro anthems "Looking for the Perfect Beat" and "Renegades of Funk," making for a potent trio of early 1980s singles.

With seminal funk collaborations "Frantic Situation" with Shango, and "Go Go Pop" with Trouble Funk, *Planet Rock: The Album* is more than mere compilation, but a veritable Rosetta Stone for understanding late 20th-century American music. Much like George Clinton's Parliament-Funkadelic saw their vision expand and multiply with the masses, these Soulsonic Force records aided in spearheading genre and cultural movements they didn't necessarily even intend.

Detroit-techno originator Juan Atkins derived inspiration from Bambaataa's work, in turn producing masterful Afrofuturist music of his own as Model 500 and other monikers. Bambaataa's records like "Looking for the Perfect Beat" ushered in not only the 1980s electro scene but also the urban Latino sound known as Freestyle. Without Bambaataa, a teenaged Andre Young might never have become Dr. Dre, whose work as part of World Class Wreckin' Cru and on early N.W.A. cuts like "Panic Zone" owes a great deal to Bambaataa's vital template. For that latter example alone, *Planet Rock: The Album* merits replay after replay.

Like this?
Check out these three too

Eric B. & Rakim
Paid in Full

Grandmaster Flash & The Furious Five
The Message

Kool Moe Dee
Kool Moe Dee

ARCADE FIRE
NEON BIBLE

by Levi J Sheppard and Joshua Lingenfelter

In early 2007, the news of a follow-up to Arcade Fire's breakout release was everywhere. At the time, Arcade Fire had already amassed such a high level of critical acclaim from *Funeral* that everyone wanted to know if they could measure up to expectations. Fans could anticipate something dark, but no one knew which direction Win Butler would focus his gaze. Before the album hit shelves, the band went on a short concert tour of churches in Ottawa, Montreal, London, and New York City, a setting that was altogether appropriate and ironic. Like the experience of listening to the album, it felt like something sacred.

Funeral was universally accepted, in spite of—or perhaps thanks to—its dark and depressing themes of personal loss; *Neon Bible* takes the listener in a different direction, defiantly exploring personal and political issues—showing believable desperation in Butler's voice when he sings, "I don't wanna work in a building downtown" on "(Antichrist Television Blues)." The songs vary in tempo and intensity, but they all stand as expressions of discontentment and rebellion. In the echo of the tragic tones of *Funeral*, *Neon Bible* moves sadness further up the emotional scale to anger, while still holding on to hopefulness. The subject matter of the songs has as much to prove to the listener as the band did to the music industry upon the album's release.

Here, the Bible is neon because the worship of advertising and materialism has become commonplace. This image serves to epitomize what this album is asking of the listener: to see the truth behind the bright lights. It's a cathartic experience; a shelter from the pressures and absurdities of modern life; somewhere to feel consoled and to take comfort in the confessions of another; a place to get angry and then to feel the relief of finding that, outside your own windowsill, things might not be so bleak. Solidifying Arcade Fire's reputation as being an honest band that sings about serious and urgent topics—a reputation that has continued to evolve well beyond the limits of their breakout efforts—*Neon Bible* is an album that proved Arcade Fire could still mine the depths of the well, for the purpose of lifting us to the lighthouse.

Like this?
Check out these three too

Islands
Return to the Sea

Talking Heads
Fear of Music

Wolf Parade
At Mount Zoomer

THE BAND
MUSIC FROM BIG PINK

by Jes Skolnik

Big Pink is a real house (yes, with siding the color of cotton candy) in West Saugerties, New York, not that far from Woodstock. It's where Bob Dylan and The Band (then Hawks, the band that backed him on his infamous 1965–6 electric tour) would write and record what would become *The Basement Tapes* while Dylan recovered from his notorious motorcycle accident. It was where The Band began to find their own independent voice, where they composed much of the lovingly named *Music from Big Pink* (for which Dylan produced the bright, naïve cover art).

Growing up the daughter of erudite hippies who are both musicians themselves, *Music from Big Pink* loomed large in my childhood. The album, which bridges nearly every genre popular with my parents' cohort at that time (rock, country, and folk, with bluesy R&B arrangements), didn't sound terribly unique or interesting to my young ears. It wasn't until I started reading about Dylan and The Band in my parents' basement library of '60s and '70s rock journalism that I realized that *Music from Big Pink* had had such an inexorable impact on so much of the "classic rock" that had come after it—Clapton's post-Cream bands, Pink Floyd, and so forth—that I was collapsing the experimental history-making template into everything it had influenced.

There's "This Wheel's on Fire," a Dylan-penned basement song that offers a grim peek into dystopian future possibilities and hinges its menace on bassist Rick Danko's serpentine playing. There's the ebullient "Chest Fever," built and carried on The Band's camaraderie, spinning out from the most structured music possible (a musical phrase from Bach's "Toccata and Fugue in D Minor") into a steady groove that breaks down in the middle and reforms. There's "The Weight," perhaps The Band's most famous song, immortalized at Woodstock and by *Easy Rider* (though contractual reasons impeded it from appearing on the soundtrack), covered by Aretha Franklin and Diana Ross—a country-folk rocker inspired by Levon Helm's own Southern upbringing and the moral quandaries at the heart of filmmaker Luis Buñuel's storytelling. *Music from Big Pink* thoroughly messes with the concepts of high and low art: it's Bach and Buñuel, it's an improvised, intuitive, wordless jamming. It's country-fried rock, deriving from Appalachian folk, and Dylan-inspired poetics. Music that began as an experiment changed the face of the rock world so thoroughly that I couldn't even recognize it as the original when I encountered it years later. No wonder my parents loved it so much.

Like this?
Check out these three too

Bob Dylan & The Band
The Basement Tapes

Bobbie Gentry
Ode to Billie Joe

Grateful Dead
American Beauty

THE BEACH BOYS
PET SOUNDS

by Cameron Schaefer

Pet Sounds is often heralded as one of the best albums ever made, but it's also one of the darkest. This may seem antithetical to the sunny, California-dreaming ethos of the Beach Boys, but that leads us to the second thing. *Pet Sounds* is not a Beach Boys album, it's a Brian Wilson album.

In December of 1964, the same year the Beatles made landfall on American soil, Wilson suffered a nervous breakdown on a flight to Houston, sobbing and screaming into a pillow. Soon after, he ceased touring with the band, vowing to stay behind and write great songs. Severed from the band, recently introduced to marijuana and LSD, witness to the separation of his parents, and desperate to create something meaningful, Wilson retreated to the studio and gave himself over completely to his music.

During this time the Beatles released *Rubber Soul*, which came to Brian as both an oracle and an expertly thrown gauntlet. Of the album Wilson said, "When I heard *Rubber Soul* I said, 'That's it. That's all. That's all, folks.' I said, 'I'm going to make an album that's really good, I mean really challenge me.' I mean, I love that fucking album, I cherish that album."

Inspired by the lack of filler in *Rubber Soul*, Wilson came into the studio with songwriting companion Tony Asher on a mission to "make the greatest rock album ever made!"

The resulting sessions—recorded mostly by the Los Angeles session wizards called The Wrecking Crew—brought forth great songs, but more importantly a multi-layered piece of art that mined Wilson's shadow self. In contrast to the somewhat frivolous cover image, and an album title that Asher felt "trivialized what [they] had accomplished," "That's Not Me," "I'm Waiting for the Day," "I Know There's an Answer," "I Just Wasn't Made for These Times" are songs whose lyrics pulse with dark doubts, and fatigue that could be as easily appropriated by teenagers experiencing their first heartbreak as it could soldiers returning home from Vietnam. The album would prove a prophetic road map for a world that would soon need to confront similar demons as the wet sheen of '60s optimism calcified.

Just prior to the album's release, it was played for John Lennon and Paul McCartney in a London hotel room where they listened once all the way through, sat quietly, and asked for it to be played again. With *Pet Sounds*, Wilson took a cacophony of sounds, instruments, and emotions and produced a universally human album; a longing, searching, desperate album. Deeply inspired by the experience, Lennon and McCartney soon began work on what would become *Sgt. Pepper's Lonely Hearts Club Band*, while *Pet Sounds* would be released a few weeks later to a lukewarm reception. Brian Wilson was 23.

Like this?
Check out these three too

The Beatles
Rubber Soul

The Beach Boys
Surf's Up

The Ronettes
...Presenting the Fabulous Ronettes Featuring Veronica

The Beach Boys Pet Sounds

Sloop John B./ Caroline No
Wouldn't It Be Nice/You Still Believe In Me
That's Not Me/Don't Talk (Put Your Head on My Shoulder)
I'm Waiting For The Day/Let's Go Away For Awhile
God Only Knows/I Know There's An Answer/Here Today
I Just Wasn't Made For These Times / Pet Sounds

BEACH HOUSE
TEEN DREAM

by Jes Skolnik

After exhaustive touring for their previous record, *Devotion*, the Baltimore dream-pop duo of Victoria Legrand and Alex Scally found themselves with a surfeit of creative ideas that they'd developed on the road together and couldn't wait to get back home to refine and record. The result, *Teen Dream*, is an expansive and diverse record that saw the duo breaking out of their previous slow, reverb-heavy, gloomy style. They spent as much money as they could on the recording and production process, trying to push themselves artistically and put as much care and intent into recording as possible.

The change in sound from *Devotion* is immediately evident upon hearing the first warm, clear, twinkling notes of *Teen Dream* opener "Zebra" and mirrored in the referential cover art. This was a significant departure in nearly every conceivable way. *Teen Dream* was recorded in a converted church in upstate New York with producer Chris Coady, and it does indeed arch toward the experience of the sublime. It's a record that sparkles and shimmers, full of air, light, and movement. Scally's guitar lines whirl like golden ribbons around Legrand's droning keyboards and twine with her smoky, languid vocal melodies. Legrand's lyrics are oblique, but never reach the kind of gossamer glossolalia pioneered by Elizabeth Fraser of the Cocteau Twins; she spins recognizable, relatable tales of isolation, loss, all-consuming romantic love, and desire. Beach House diversify their ethereal sound here; there is pure pop on this record ("Walk in the Park"), even moments recalling Fleetwood Mac's early '80s crystalline hits ("Lover of Mine"). When they do drift into ambient melancholy ("10 Mile Stereo"), it is redolent with pulsing tension. On some more delicate and spacious moments ("Take Care," "Better Times") there are instrumental and stylistic nods to folk, country, and soul.

Teen Dream was an immediate fan and critical favorite, making many publications' "best of" lists for the year and the decade. It catapulted Beach House from a niche, locally based fan favorite to real indie-rock stardom.

Like this? Check out these three too

Broadcast
The Noise Made by People

Celebration
The Modern Tribe

Mazzy Star
So Tonight That I Might See

BEASTIE BOYS
PAUL'S BOUTIQUE

by Chris Lay

By nature of its length and breadth, ranking the Beastie Boys discography is intensely subjective. Sure, *Paul's Boutique* might not be your personal-favorite album of theirs (they definitely have a few other albums that are equally legit "masterpiece" contenders), but it's almost inarguable at this point that their second album is their most artful in its conception and execution. Despite their massive album sales, Mike D, MCA, and Ad-Rock were quickly burning through the gleefully immature "Fight for Your Right" frat-rap persona established by their debut album *Licensed to Ill*, so they headed out to Los Angeles to clear their heads and record a follow-up.

From a production standpoint, this album could never get made today for legal reasons. The years before Gilbert O'Sullivan fleeced Biz Markie in court over flipping "Alone Again (Naturally)" were simpler times, where you could get away with liberally sprinkling bits and pieces from a hundred or more songs all over your album with minimal hassle from lawyers. With the mysterious Matt Dike behind the boards tossing everything but the kitchen sink at the boys—from Superfly to Loggins and Messina to the damn *Jaws* theme—the trio broke open and dropped some of their most densely referential rhymes. "Hey Ladies," for example, puts Magilla Gorilla, Timothy Leary, Chuck Woolery, Vincent van Gogh,

and Japanese baseball player Sadaharu Oh in the same room, all rubbing shoulders and competing for the attention of the ladies in question . . . and this is the lead single?! Living up to its title, *Paul's Boutique* bites liberally from McCartney himself when the whole affair ends with "B-Boy Bouillabaisse," a 12- minute opus that, across its nine movements, rips a conceptual page from the back of the Bible that is *Abbey Road* and rolls a fat spliff with it.

Rap as a genre had been around for more than a decade, and while *Paul's Boutique* wasn't the first truly transcendent rap album, it was the first to really explode its borders, coloring outside of the lines and jotting notes in the margins at the same time. It's a throwback to the days before sampling laws clamped down on producers, making rap records on that scale financially untenable, but it looks forward to what rap could be and documents the moment when the trio became much more than the sum of their parts.

It is a credit to the album's cult status that the intersection of Ludlow Street and Rivington, which features on the panoramic photo on the album's artwork, has become something of a tourist spot for music-lovers today. Jeremy Shatan, the Beastie Boys' former bandmate in the Young Aborigines, took the now famous image, although it is credited to the nom de plume of the band, Nathanial Hörnblowér.

Like this?
Check out these three too

**Brand Nubian
One for All**

**De La Soul
3 Feet High
and Rising**

**Prince Paul
Psychoanalysis:
What Is It?**

THE BEATLES
SGT. PEPPER'S LONELY HEARTS CLUB BAND

by Eric Sundermann

The Beatles' *Sgt. Pepper's Lonely Hearts Club Band* is widely regarded as the greatest album of all time by a band that's widely regarded as the greatest rock band of all time. This was the eighth studio album from the Beatles, and the influence of its bold exploration of concept and songwriting has been felt in nearly every piece of music that's been recorded since. Gone were the silly little love songs from Paul McCartney and John Lennon that made the Beatles the biggest band the world had ever seen and the four most eligible bachelors on planet Earth.

Instead, here we had 13 songs—none of which was a single, by the way—attempting to redefine what it means to make a rock album in a time when the genre was barely old enough to drink coffee. The endeavor was successful, as *Sgt. Pepper's* would go on to be the first rock album to win the Grammy for Album of the Year, and introduced the world to the idea of the concept album and what that could be as an artistic expression. It attempted to show that high-minded, complicated music could be presented in a pop-friendly manner, not restricted to the genres of jazz or classical.

The simple idea to present the group as a phony live-performance band shaped everything about the record—looking at more than just the recordings, but also the recording process and the way it packaged itself. Everything felt calculated and purposeful, which was a new idea that would set the tone for decades to come. Even half a century later, much of the motivation for the manner in which artists release music can be traced back to those stupid outfits that look like they escaped from a locked closet in Las Vegas.

Like this?
Check out these three too

The Beach Boys
Smiley Smile

George Harrison
All Things Must Pass

Harry Nilsson
Nilsson Schmilsson

31

BECK
SEA CHANGE

by Eric Sundermann

Existence is hard. The day-to-day monotony of everyday life can be more draining than any other obstacle we face as human beings. What is it about waking up that can feel so grueling? Why does the alarm sound so terrible? How can we manage to be unhappy when we live in a time that's more advanced than any other in human history? Beck's *Sea Change*—the musician's beautifully basic, fifth official studio album that's an exploration of emotional struggle—is this postmodern sentiment to life set to music.

Written after the end of a relationship that lasted nine years, Beck takes the very straightforward experience of having your heart *fucking broken* and ruminates on it for 52 minutes. Rumor is that he wrote most of the record on an acoustic guitar in about a week, right after the relationship ended (due to his significant other being unfaithful), but then shelved the songs before recording, allowing them to age like a fine wine. Once they were eventually put to tape and the album was released, listeners were surprised to experience a new Beck. Gone were the ironic and self-aware lyrics of his previous work—replaced with bare, melancholic lyrics that weren't anything except really, really sad. The added element of Jeremy Blake, the artist behind the ethereally hopeful cover art, dying by suicide by walking into the Atlantic Ocean makes the whole thing a bit crushing either to listen to or think about.

But what makes *Sea Change* a classic record isn't how it came to exist, or how he used it to change the sonic direction of his career. Instead, it's how Beck was able to capture such a specific and complicated emotion on tape, somehow both embracing and challenging the clichés that come with heartbreak. Let's be real: is there any worse feeling in the world than when someone tells you they don't love you anymore? Somehow, *Sea Change* feels hopeless by being fearless. There's nothing more human than that.

Like this?
Check out these three too

**Nick Drake
Pink Moon
(see pages 82–3)**

**Serge Gainsbourg
Histoire de
Melody Nelson**

**Harry Nilsson
Son of
Schmilsson**

BEYONCÉ

BEYONCÉ BEYONCÉ

by Caitlin White

Beyoncé opens with a black woman's affirmation of her own personal happiness, building from there toward an explicitly personal revelation of marital bliss, sexuality, and unflinching, unexpected feminism. The phrase "world-stopping" is usually hyperbole, but in this case it really wasn't; the surprise release of Beyoncé's fifth record in late 2013 forever changed the way the industry conceived of major-label album releases. A number of high-profile artists attempted to pull off the same feat after this record came out, but most failed miserably.

That's the thing about Beyoncé though: many people try to imitate what she does, but there is no one else who could make a slurred pronunciation of "surfbordt" into a declaration of sly, sexual ecstasy so iconic it managed to eclipse the questionable Jay Z verse that followed on the album's obvious lead single, "Drunk in Love." File that one next to the explosive power ballad "XO" and her personal-is-political strut "***Flawless"

as three of the album's standout tracks.

It might be hard to remember back before this record dropped, but Beyoncé's place in the pop-star ecosystem wasn't a given like it is now. Sure, she was a popular singer who routinely performed to stadium-size crowds, but the near ubiquitous adoration she receives now is directly tied to the success of her self-titled release; its cover art demonstrated the lack of necessity for adornment, and designer Todd Tourso provided what he called a "subversion of femininity" with the grey-pink hued font. From the searing sexuality of "Rocket" or "Blow" to the slinky "No Angel" or vaunting "Partition," Beyoncé flexes between her R&B diva chops and a fascination with rap's churning beats and eternal stunting.

It's important to have this album on vinyl because of what a monumental accomplishment it was in Beyoncé's career, but make sure to get the digital version, too, for the slew of gorgeous and compelling videos that accompanied its release.

Like this? Check out these three too

Janet Jackson
Control

Janelle Monáe
The ArchAndroid

Solange
True

BIG STAR
#1 RECORD

by Susannah Young

The story of Big Star is a microcosm of the way anything resembling progress always happens in Memphis: sparking through shared connections; gaining momentum through a community's generosity with their time, talent, and resources; blossoming through a grassroots effort to work together, make something cool, and see what happens on the other side. It's sad that this boots-on-the-ground approach ultimately stems from disinterest, disinvestment, and corruption—but the one upside of living in a place where the people in power aren't willing to invest in your progress is that people get to define for *themselves* what progress looks like. It's why I regularly saw Al Kapone at my neighborhood's farmers' market; why all the 60-something white ladies at my job wore wifebeaters that said "Get Crunk" the day after Three 6 Mafia won an Oscar; why the *Washington Post* deems the Memphis Grizzlies' vibrant fandom worth covering at a national level. Why the album art for *#1 Record* says as much about the context of Big Star as it does their name. Memphis is a community built from the ground up, not the top down.

But Memphis *also* has a history of letting its own brand of dysfunction compromise its best intentions—and the story of Big Star follows apace. *#1 Record* should have been exactly that, but creative friction between Alex Chilton and Chris Bell, Stax Records' bungled distribution deal, and critical acclaim without popular acceptance conspired to shove Big Star and *#1 Record* to the Back Burner of Music History

for decades on end. Which is why *#1 Record* feels like an encapsulation of a brief moment in time when everything was working exactly as it should. The only Big Star album officially featuring Chris Bell (though his fingerprints are all over *Radio City*)—he left the band and died in a car crash just six years after *#1 Record* came out. The knockout punch sequencing of "The Ballad of El Goodo," "In the Street," and "Thirteen." The map of all the band's influences (the Beatles, the Byrds, among others) reframed as something new and dynamic. And the songs themselves, which chronicle and crystallize a fleeting time in our lives: the in-betweenness of adolescence, when you think you're ready to experience more than you're actually ready to experience (and you know it but ignore it anyway); exploring the boundaries of your feelings for another person without knowing how to navigate that terrain; whining about being bored immediately before indulging in an existential crisis dark beyond your years.

Listen to *#1 Record* because "Would you be an outlaw for my love?" is the English language's most simultaneously teen-dumb and swoon-worthy question. Listen to *#1 Record* so you can tell people "In the Street" isn't a Cheap Trick song. Listen to *#1 Record* because it represents the creative output of a city whose greatest asset is its appetite for—and history of—creating connections that produce paradigm-shifting art. Listen to *#1 Record* because it should have been the beginning of something that never got to be.

Like this?
Check out these three too

Badfinger
No Dice

Cheap Trick
Cheap Trick at Budokan

The Modern Lovers
The Modern Lovers

DIAMOND BACK

Ingredients

1½ fl oz (45ml) rye whiskey
(such as Rittenhouse)

¾ fl oz (20ml) applejack
(such as Laird's)

¾ fl oz (20ml) green chartreuse

ice

cherry, to garnish (optional)

Method

Combine all the ingredients in an ice-filled mixing glass. Stir for 30 seconds then strain into a chilled cocktail glass. Garnish with a cherry . . . or not, it's your drink! If it's too sweet, dial back the chartreuse a bit next time.

BIKINI KILL
BIKINI KILL

by Chris Lay

Sure, capitalism schmapitalism or whatever, but there's definitely something to be said for a free market correcting itself. In the 15 or so years since its inception, punk rock had become an epic sausage fest. With next to zero bands with even a single lady in them, much less a majority, Bikini Kill kicked off a whole movement when Kathleen Hanna opened their Ian MacKaye-produced, self-titled EP by screeching (after a false start of course), "We're Bikini Kill, and we want revolution girl-style now!" It tipped the hardcore scales back at least a little bit toward a healthier gender balance with the Riot Grrrl movement they helped foster. Tammy Rae Carland, fellow Riot Grrrl member, produced the zine-style album artwork for *Bikini Kill*, capturing the band's exuberant lack of self-consciousness.

With its roots in Olympia, Washington's zine culture, Bikini Kill was founded by Kathleen Hanna, Tobi Vail, and Kathi Wilcox, who later added Billy Karren on guitar. Their shows were known for their singer going above and beyond the call to reclaim shows as explicitly safe (and FUN) spaces for women, handing out lyric sheets for singalongs, making sure things didn't get too rough, and booting out dudes who couldn't handle getting bumped down the totem pole.

"Feels Blind" is maybe the best example of what a profound punk-rock Trojan horse Bikini Kill had created with this pervasive reclamation mentality. Brazenly poetic lyrics like "All the doves that fly past my eyes/Have a stickiness to their wings/In the doorway of my demise I stand/Encased in the whisper you taught me" aggressively mark their territory when placed so pointedly in the context of such a fast and hard album. While their politics were no joke, Bikini Kill didn't take *everything* so seriously. The last track on the album, "Thurston Hearts the Who," hearkens back to their zine-style roots with a reading of a review of the band and with lyrics that mocked the way Thurston Moore's approval was such a pointless aspiration.

If the origins of punk rock were a total "fuck you" to norms and expectations, Bikini Kill was the powerful and necessary corrective force that re-opened the door for bands like Bratmobile, Sleater-Kinney, and L7, all the way up to Pussy Riot. Like every good war cry, though, the music's gotta be worth it. Even at a tight 15 minutes, *Bikini Kill* packs more punch per second than just about any other album out there.

Like this?
Check out these three too

Bratmobile
Pottymouth

The Gossip
Standing in the Way of Control

Sleater-Kinney
The Woods

THE BLACK KEYS
THICKFREAKNESS

by Cameron Schaefer

Thickfreakness was the second album from childhood friends Dan Auerbach and Patrick Carney, the blues-rock duo who had dropped out of college and formed the Black Keys just one year prior. They were signed to Fat Possum following a well-received debut album, *The Big Come Up*, though their ties with the label had actually come about a few years earlier when Dan drove down to Mississippi with his father after expressing interest in learning from some of the last remaining Delta-blues men.

"Junior Kimbrough had passed, and R.L. Burnside was on tour, so we directed him down to Greenville to visit T-Model Ford," explained Fat Possum's GM, Bruce Watson. "Dan's dad dropped his son off at the trailer of T-Model Ford with his guitar and an apt pupil's energy. The next day his father came and picked him up, and they drove home."

Recorded in one 14-hour session, *Thick-freakness* captured the raw, lo-fi frenzy of Auerbach and Carney as they channeled the energy of artists who knew they'd tapped into something much bigger, choosing to keep the tapes rolling so as not to let the magic flee before they could pin it down for 11 tracks. Carney pounds the drums like a manic, hammer-slinging Thor, and Auerbach's voice and guitar melt into cigarette smoke only to coalesce in the roof of his mouth as gravel waiting to be spit. The whole thing is perfect.

In 1992, when Fat Possum and music critic Robert Palmer managed to pin down Junior Kimbrough for a night to record him in his Marshall County juke joint, a similar magic took place, resulting in the critically acclaimed *All Night Long*. It's unlikely the Black Keys set out to intentionally re-create this recording session, but if one spends much time with the blues, you find these seemingly rushed, raw sessions make up much of the canon. Robert Johnson in a hotel room, Lead Belly in the Parchman Farm penitentiary, Junior in his juke joint, and the two boys from Akron in a basement.

Like this?
Check out these three too

**Deadboy & The Elephantmen
We Are
Night Sky**

**Junior Kimbrough
Most Things
Haven't
Worked Out**

**The White Stripes
De Stijl**

JAMES BLAKE
JAMES BLAKE

by Tyler Barstow

It's not impossible for a band to be good during a late afternoon or early evening set at a festival, but it's unlikely. Pretty much everything is stacked against them. Most of the crowd is teetering on heatstroke and careening through the uncomfortable final section of the day-drinking roller coaster and, unless one of the sound guys is Merlin, the important parts of the mix seem to come out of the speakers tied to balloons. People are wiped out, and it's not for the faint of heart. It's been done well, though, and perhaps the best example I've seen was James Blake back in 2014 at Governors Ball. James Blake crashed onto the scene in 2011 with his self-titled debut, and he's become something of a benevolent musical Midas since then, which is to say that nearly everything he touches becomes incredible without ruining any lives.

His creative bent is fixed on causing listeners and objects to levitate, and the easiest way to explain why you should listen to him is that he's a Frankenstein's monster who D'Angelo and Thom Yorke created together. He's half R&B, half exploratory synth astronaut, and the albums he's brought back to earth are some of the most important to be released over the last five years or so. He has a singular way of commanding your mood/attention/playlist unexpectedly, and that was abundantly clear that day in New York. Along with proving he's one of the only white people allowed to cover Bill Withers, he took the 500-plus crowd to church without asking anyone's permission when he closed with "Measurements," a song that would be equally at home in a cathedral or pumping out of a Brooklyn jukebox.

Much like Justin Vernon of Bon Iver and his debut album *For Emma, Forever Ago*, this album is when James Blake became, well, James Blake. It finds him at the beginning of his more public creative arc, and full of the muffled clairvoyance that's come to define him as an artist since its release. Even the cover art speaks to the sense of mystery and self-abandonment that sits at the center of his work. It's the first major work of one of our generation's quietest, and most essential, artists and one of the birthplaces of modern hermit soul. Put it on your shelf next to Nick Drake and Marvin Gaye, and take it down from that shelf and play it as often as you possibly can.

Like this?
Check out these three too

Antony and the Johnsons
I Am a Bird Now

Mount Kimbie
Crooks & Lovers

Thom Yorke
The Eraser

Listen to with...

CAPRICE

Ingredients

1 ½ fl oz (45ml) gin

½ fl oz (15ml) dry vermouth

½ fl oz (15ml) Benedictine

dash of orange bitters

ice

Method

Put all the ingredients into a
mixing glass and stir to combine.
Strain into a chilled coupe glass
and serve.

BON IVER
BON IVER

by Tyler Hayes

From the backcountry woods, pounding on an acoustic guitar, to often thick synth sounds and electronic elements, Justin Vernon further exposed the constants of his Bon Iver project with the self-titled follow-up to *For Emma, Forever Ago*. Both albums, played back-to-back, are seemingly far apart musically, but they are different ends of the same forest. Vernon's storytelling is the trunk of a tree; and both albums are branches facing opposite directions.

Lyrically, *Bon Iver* is just as tortured as *For Emma, Forever Ago*. It's a record full of despair. Maybe that's one reason it doesn't feel like it ultimately strays too far from the last album. One of the weirdest examples of where some of the grief comes from is how the first track, "Perth," was influenced by Heath Ledger's death—something Vernon told *Rolling Stone* in 2011.

There's a cohesiveness to this record even beyond the song-naming convention, the lyrics, or the music. Plenty of albums get at least one of those things right. This one gets those all to work together. For better or worse, it's an album that demands to be swallowed whole—as songs glide from one to the next. From a soft beginning, the dynamic sound arc in the track listing is a thing of beauty. *Bon Iver* should fit in most people's daily circumstance. It's an easy album to throw on at different times, no matter what. Still, the album's tone is one that comes alive at night, whether on a long drive or playing on home speakers while having a couple of friends over.

If ever there were a perfect conclusion to a group of songs, "Beth/Rest" is that great ending. It's a montage-inducing slow jam. It takes the right final song to make you want to reach over, press play, and start the journey over again; "Beth/Rest" does just that.

Like this? Check out these three too

Destroyer
Kaputt

Bruce Hornsby and the Range
The Way It Is

Iron and Wine
The Creek Drank the Cradle

THE BOOKS
THE LEMON OF PINK

by Luke Winkie

When the Books broke up back in 2012 they issued a box set titled, somewhat modestly, *A Dot in Time*. That title always seemed very fitting; the partnership between guitarist Nick Zammuto and cellist Paul de Jong was always lumped into the same early-2000s art scene that produced bands like the Yeah Yeah Yeahs and Animal Collective, which was a distinction that seemed to exist mostly because they were written about in the same magazines. But while the Books shared the same fans and rode the same wave, they always seemed a little apart from everything else. They were more idea than band; a smart combination of pristine samples from language tapes, in-flight announcements, and other cultural debris with their own significant virtuosity. Nothing sounded quite like them, which was exactly the point.

Their second album, *The Lemon of Pink*, is their best and most song-oriented work. The Books had a unique way of satisfying desires you didn't know existed. In the album's standout, "Tokyo," a mind-boggling guitar pattern morphs into a cello, and then a computer hemorrhage, and back into a guitar again. In "There Is No There," a phased, microscopic string orchestra joins the guidance of some long-forgotten voice that's been regurgitated again and again through Pro Tools wizardry till it sounds like a choir. Critics coined the term "folktronica," a reductive non-genre, to try and make sense of the Books' world, but that decidedly missed the point.

We're never going to hear another album quite like *The Lemon of Pink* again. Why? Because we're never going to witness another coincidence quite like a transcendent guitarist meeting a transcendent cellist who both happen to have major crushes on Aphex Twin, DJ Shadow, and public-access fragments. No band will ever be founded on these principles ever again, and we should devour this dot in time while we still can. We should be grateful.

Like this?
Check out these three too

**The Avalanches
Since I Left You**

**The Notwist
The Notwist**

**The United States
of America
The United States
of America**

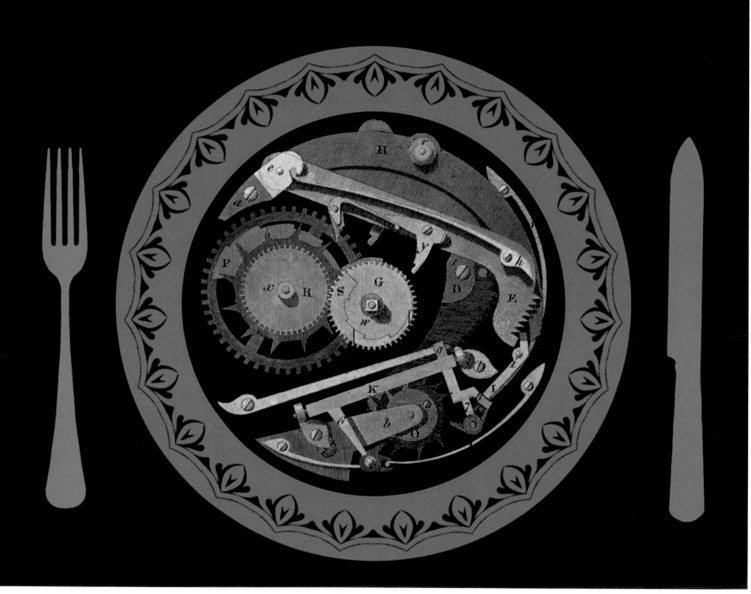

DAVID BOWIE
"HEROES"

by Andrew Winistorfer

When David Bowie died after a long battle with cancer in early 2016, it was the final death of an artist who had made the invention and death of his various personae central to his identity as a pop star. There was the folkie of "Space Oddity," the space alien and his endlessly replicated alter ego (Ziggy Stardust and Aladdin Sane), the Thin White Duke, and the New Romantic Bowie of the early '80s and "Ashes to Ashes."

"Heroes" is from one of the most underrated eras of Bowie's career, his *The Man Who Fell to Earth* era. It's the centerpiece to his so-called Berlin Trilogy—sandwiched as it is between *Low* and *Lodger*—albums Bowie made in Europe after fleeing his drug problems and Los Angeles. Bowie was coming down from cocaine in Berlin, but he was also coming down from being one of the biggest pop stars of the post-Beatles era. Instead of trying to top the successes of his Thin White Duke "plastic soul" albums, he retreated to Europe to make weirdo art-rock records with Brian Eno. Like the mime-artist pose he strikes on the cover of *"Heroes"*, Bowie was ready to change visage once more.

While *Low* placed Bowie over the shattered noise and ambient music on which Brian Eno was working at the time—there was hardly a guitar to be found—*"Heroes"* expanded Eno's palette to include the fretboard melting of Robert Fripp, who was on loan from King Crimson. Most of the songs on *"Heroes"* were allegedly recorded in single takes, with Bowie and Eno working on the same wavelength. From the opening piano strokes and gnarled guitar electrics of "Beauty and the Beast" to the wild drums of "The Secret Life of Arabia," *"Heroes"* is bursting at the seams with daring sounds and experimentation.

Of course, any discussion of *"Heroes"* the album has to get around to "Heroes" the song, the one Bowie song that will be played in video packages for sports teams forever. Written about a couple falling in love in the shadow of the Berlin Wall, "Heroes" is a totemic song that never even comes to an end. It builds and builds and builds and just fades out. *"Heroes"* was never the commercial smash RCA probably wanted from Bowie at the time—the title track hardly charted—but it's one of his most essential albums. It's the sound of an artist who always pushed himself to be different persona-wise, completely changing his musical persona too.

Like this?
Check out these three too

Brian Eno
Here Come the Warm Jets

Peter Gabriel
So

King Crimson
Islands

BURIAL ✕
UNTRUE. HDBLP002

BURIAL
UNTRUE

by Gary Suarez

Few records ever truly tap into the Zeitgeist in any meaningful way. Naturally, commercial successes can hold personal sentimental value, something to which many Adele devotees can attest. But an album that captures our collective feeling at a given time is something more than special. So when something as left-field and unconventional as Burial's second album, *Untrue*, connects as deeply into culture as it did, further investigation is warranted.

Untrue came six years after 9/11 and four years into the Iraq War, with a new generation bearing witness nightly to dystopia and new millennial doom on our screens after years of perceived peace through rose-colored blinders. The economies of the industrialized were suffering through a financial crisis and looming recession, with negative impact on young entrants into the workforce. First-world problems, perhaps, but it all ran counter to what had been promised to an age group that grew up in a time of less conflict and more prosperity.

On top of all that, people were encouraged to go about their lives, to consume and mingle, and even love. Perhaps that's why Ray J's sampled moan on "Archangel" resonates as much as it does, the inherent urges and longings unspooling over crackling atmospheres, muted rhythms, and surging pads. There's beauty and sorrow to tracks like "Endorphin" or "Etched Headplate," providing a tenebrous soundtrack to depression or desperation with a hopeful undercurrent occasionally present. Soul abstractions pervade the record, with "Shell of Light" one of *Untrue*'s most gripping moments.

Burial's deliberate facelessness (although he was eventually "outed" in 2008 as William Bevan) made him convenient for many of us to identify with, and song titles like "In McDonalds" made his cryptic work more relatable than most electronic music. Yet that anonymity prompted a desire for unmasking among his curious fans, a craving to see if he truly was one of us. The tenuous musical connection to UK garage and dubstep gave Burial a presumed country of origin, and the eventual selfie presented an ordinary man, unsmiling over this compulsory reveal. We broke an unspoken covenant with Burial, and the subsequent slowing of his recorded output appears to affirm that. To better understand him and ourselves, we thankfully still have his masterpiece.

Like this?
Check out these three too

**Craig David
Born to Do It**

**Dizzee Rascal
Boy in
da Corner**

**Slipmatt
Slipmatt 25**

CAPTAIN BEEFHEART & HIS MAGIC BAND TROUT MASK REPLICA

by Donivan Berube

This is a sound that takes time, a style that you have to ease into over the years before finding that moment of clarity where all of the nonsense falls suddenly into place. Marc Maron has a great standup bit about it, saying, "I will never be smart enough, or large enough of mind, to assess and understand Captain Beefheart."

Imagine Jim Morrison's birthday party happening in the next hotel room, and you're sitting up all night with your ear glued to the wall. Think less of the band name and more of the man: a true artist by definition, a child prodigy melting away in a Mojave Desert trailer park. Don Van Vliet started the band with his school friend Frank Zappa, the two spending their time spinning records together and studying the music of blues-guitar legends like Robert Johnson and Howlin' Wolf. The third Beefheart record, *Trout Mask Replica*—with its gloriously literal accompanying artwork—is their critically professed masterpiece, but somehow also their hardest bit of listening, an indescribable swan dive into the unholy weird. Side one alone goes from the sharpened riff rock of "Frownland" to the echoing spoken word of "The Dust Blows Forward 'n the Dust Blows Back," and

guitar-led free jazz in "Dachau Blues." All throughout is an even mixture of every possible genre, from a strange bit of the blues to the unpredictably avant-garde.

Despite their potential, the band never seemed destined for the mainstream success that the industry had dreamed up for them. Just one week before their expected breakthrough at the famed Monterey International Pop Festival, Vliet was so overwhelmed with LSD that he looked out into the audience, straightened his tie, and stepped clear off the 10-foot-high stage, later explaining that he'd seen a girl in the audience turn into a fish, bubbles floating out of her mouth, and he simply wanted to talk to her. This caused their young virtuoso guitarist Ry Cooder to quit, and from then Vliet couldn't help but to make one left turn after another, chasing his own tail into a blank map of musicality.

Trout Mask Replica may not be much of an icebreaker, but given enough attention it remains the centerpiece to the band's lasting legacy. Someday you get to feeling just weird enough for it all to come together. In Vliet's own words: "If you want to be a different fish, you've got to jump out of the school."

Like this?
Check out these three too

Captain Beefheart & his Magic Band
Safe as Milk

Tom Waits
Swordfishtrombones

The Mothers of Invention
Freak Out!

TROUT MASK REPLICA

CAPTAIN BEEFHEART
& HIS MAGIC BAND

THE CHILLS
KALEIDOSCOPE WORLD

by Matthew Davis

Kaleidoscope World is the starting point for the Chills, the story of how it all began and an insight into the world of New Zealand guitar pop and the "Dunedin sound"—an influence that carries on to indie-pop bands around the world today. Originally released in 1986, the compilation captures the best of the magical early-period recordings of the Chills and, much like its odd but magnetic cover art, oozes excitement and possibility.

The world's first look at the Chills came via the 1982 *Dunedin Double* compilation—featuring four acts (the Chills, the Verlaines, Sneaky Feelings, and the Stones), who all hailed from the New Zealand city in the deep south. Recorded on a portable 4-track, it was distinctly lo-fi and in tune with the DIY ethic at the heart of the burgeoning Flying Nun label.

It was a sound in part born out of geography and location, with the spaciousness and remoteness of New Zealand matched with the glowing songs of chief Chill Martin Phillipps, a music savant who somehow wrangles psychedelic pop and folk, Syd Barrett and Brian Wilson, all with Phillipps's (and much of New Zealand guitar pop's) innate ability to sound both joyous and sad within a moment.

The Chills were one of the early Flying Nun bands to make their way overseas in the '80s, and the first UK voyage resulted in UK indie Creation Records also picking up the release of *Kaleidoscope World*. It's no surprise with the neo-'60s guitar wave sitting perfectly with the label, but what was initially eight songs (later expanded to 18 and then most recently to 24) have a unique bittersweet innocence from the title track through to the happy-sad aura of "Frantic Drift" and "Rolling Moon," while the live B-side "Flame Thrower" shows a more aggressive, though still Barrett-infused, Chills.

And among all the fragile melodies mixed with a childlike wonder is "Pink Frost"—for many the Chills' most beloved track—an eerie, haunting song, and the band's first hit; the Flying Nun equivalent of "Love Will Tear Us Apart." Surrounded by the aura of death, following a dream Phillipps had, it also touches on a sense of desolation and yearning for a connection to the wider world, and there is no better example of the marvelous songwriting ability of this band from the world's southernmost point.

As Flying Nun Records founder Roger Shepherd put it, *Kaleidoscope World* is "complex, varied, but simple and direct. Musically sophisticated, but joyous, poppy, and accessible. Essential."

Like this?
Check out these three too

Syd Barrett
The Madcap Laughs

The Bats
Daddy's Highway

Saint Etienne
Foxbase Alpha

THE CLASH
LONDON CALLING

by Tom Breihan

Punk rock was a negation. Especially in its early British form, punk was about ripping down everything around it—all the fripperies and pretenses and excesses that had transformed rock music into something other than a primal energy blast. That was most famously true for the Sex Pistols, whose collective sneer burned like fire. But it was also true for the early Clash, whose self-titled debut was a fast, tinny, vital burst of antipathy: "London's burning with boredom now." The cover image—voted the best rock 'n' roll photograph of all time by *Q* magazine—symbolizes that destructively disillusioned energy, with Paul Simonon captured mid-guitar-smash.

But once you've torn the world apart, how do you put it back together again? Or as Joe Strummer howled on "Clampdown": "What are we gonna do now?" The Clash recorded their third album at the dawn of the '80s, and they spent its sprawling double-LP length fashioning a whole new sound-world from the charred scraps of whatever they thought was cool: rockabilly, reggae, cowboy movies, northern-soul horn stabs, Cadillacs.

The Clash of *London Calling* didn't sound much like a punk band anymore, at least not in the context of 1979 London. But they didn't sound like a rock band either. Instead, they were something new. They took all those shards of culture and fashioned them into a big, joyous, life-affirming mountain of sound. On "Rudie Can't Fail" they beat the then-current UK ska revival at its own game. On "The Guns of Brixton" they mastered dub reggae foreboding better than any other white rockers ever would. On "Death or Glory" they more or less invented Big Country's '80s anthem rock. And on and on, every song revealing a whole new side of the people who made it.

But it wasn't *just* a blast, and that's mostly because of Joe Strummer, a singer who couldn't help but sound like he was wrapped in electrified barbed wire. While the music may have been utopian, Strummer's voice and lyrics took various global calamities and transformed them into an all-consuming, directionless anxiety. No surprise that Mick Jones, Strummer's co-writer, was the one who sang the album's catchiest songs, "Lost in the Supermarket" and "Train in Vain," both of which anticipated the new wave that would soon take over. (It remains crazy that a solid-gold hit like "Train in Vain" was once an unlisted bonus track.) On *London Calling*, they sounded like a party at the end of the world, dread hanging heavy over the whole celebration.

Like this? Check out these three too

The Jam
The Gift

The Sex Pistols
Never Mind the Bollocks, Here's the Sex Pistols

Television
Marquee Moon

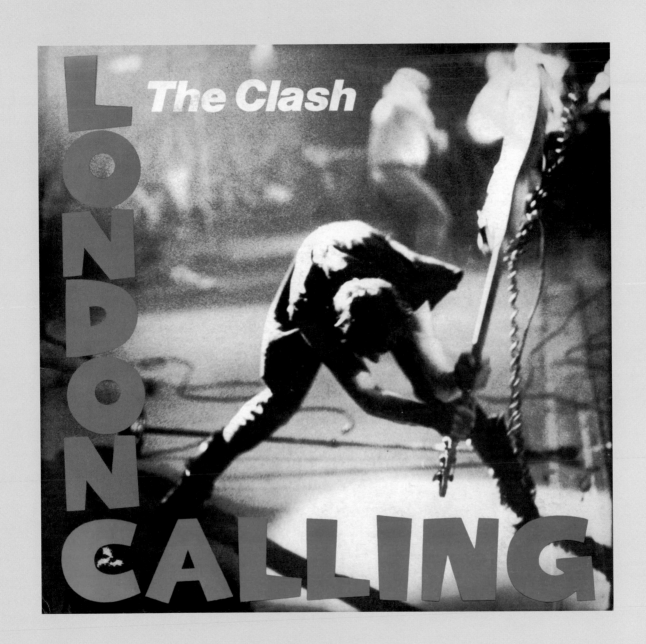

CLIPSE
LORD WILLIN'

by Andrew Winistorfer

Clipse's *Lord Willin'* is certified platinum for selling more than a million copies in the US, but if you based album certifications on how often a beat has been pounded out on a lunch table, *Lord Willin'* and "Grindin'" would be at least "lunch-table double diamond." Even people who are only vaguely aware that Kanye's drug-dealer best friend Pusha T used to be in a group can bang out the skeletal beat from "Grindin'."

Lord Willin' is Clipse's debut, but it wasn't supposed to be. Friends of Pharrell Williams from way back, Pusha T and No Malice got signed to an Elektra Records deal in 1996 during the post-Biggie/Tupac major-label rap gold rush. The 1999 Neptunes-produced album they recorded for Elektra, *Exclusive Audio Footage*, was shelved immediately when the lead single, "The Funeral," failed to light up the rap charts. Elektra dropped the group, and *Exclusive* became the rap-music version of the Beach Boys' *Smile*.

Pharrell took Clipse with him to Arista, and set to work on *Lord Willin'*, producing the whole thing with his Neptunes partner Chad Hugo. It can't be said enough how important the Neptunes are to *Lord Willin'*; Pharrell and Chad knew that the stone-cold cocaine tales that Pusha and Malice weave were best augmented by minimal beats with oozing synths and lacerating organs. *Lord Willin'* is a perfect melding of producer and rappers, an achievement of hip-hop album craft.

"Grindin'" sometimes feels like the nucleus of *Lord Willin'*, but in some ways that's one track earlier. The crawling "Virginia" builds Clipse's native Virginia as a desperate place, where he needs to keep "chrome close to my bones," and "ain't shit to do but cook" cocaine, and where being humble gets you no respect. "Ironic, the same place I'm making figures at/That there's the same land they used to hang n****s at," Malice raps, summing up in two lines the hidden politics of Clipse and the reality of urbanization in the post-slavery South.

Clipse will never get enough credit for being funny—this album's cover with the group riding with Jesus is hysterical. "When the Last Time" was the album's club hit, and "Young Boy" and "Cot' Damn" became unlikely commercial bumper music, but it all comes back to "Grindin'," a song that still sounds like 3002 as much as it does 2002. It's the best rap song of the 21st century, and that alone makes *Lord Willin'* essential. That the rest of the album lives up to "Grindin'," is, like Malice's raw demeanor, icing on the cake.

Like this?
Check out these three too

**Big Daddy Kane
Long Live
the Kane**

**Schoolly D
Schoolly D**

**Young Jeezy
Let's Get It: Thug
Motivation 101**

JOHN COLTRANE
A LOVE SUPREME

by Andrew Martin

The importance of an album like *A Love Supreme* cannot be overstated. There are other works in John Coltrane's undeniable catalog that can be called seminal and even groundbreaking (note: *Blue Train* and *Giant Steps* are both incredible). But it's *A Love Supreme* that resonates the strongest, both because of its arrangements and its sentiments.

There's not a second wasted in the album's runtime of just over 33 minutes. The solos are dizzying spells of instrumental wizardry, particularly Elvin Jones's flooring drum solo at the outset of "Pursuance." On the vinyl copy, you're treated to his standout moment after flipping to side two, where pianist McCoy Tyner speeds and clanks across his keys, and Jimmy Garrison absolutely goes off on his double bass. These are four crazy-talented artists at their arguable primes *playing on the same record*—something we should consider ourselves lucky to hear.

A Love Supreme is more than its wealth of astounding instrumentation. It's rooted in Coltrane's spirituality, which he explores in the liner notes and had explained in a number of interviews. After years spent battling substance abuse (heroin and alcohol), he overcame his addictions through finding peace in religion, a sentiment anyone who's studied most major religions will tell you is the basis of all of them. It also helped birth "spiritual jazz," a sub-genre that includes everyone from Pharoah Sanders to Kamasi Washington (whose 2015 release, *The Epic*, is a modern masterpiece that reaffirmed that jazz is, indeed, still cool).

But here's the thing: *A Love Supreme*'s spirituality isn't overbearing, judgmental, or contrived. The reflective intensity on Coltrane's face in the portrait on the cover seems a statement of intent for an album that proves soothing, reassuring, and wise. The album title itself even becomes a mantra on "Part I: Acknowledgement," with Coltrane repeatedly chanting, "a love supreme." It's an equally powerful and simple moment, a recurring dose of peace amid a musical masterpiece anchored by truly magnificent playing. If you haven't listened to *A Love Supreme* yet, I envy you, because there are few things better than hearing this record for the first time.

Like this? Check out these three too

Ornette Coleman
The Shape of Jazz to Come

Miles Davis
Kind of Blue

Sonny Rollins
The Bridge

SLOE GIN FIZZ

Ingredients

2 fl oz (60ml) sloe gin

½ fl oz (15ml) fresh lemon juice

1 teaspoon superfine (caster) sugar

club soda (soda water)

ice

Method

Half fill a cocktail shaker with ice and stir in the gin, lemon juice, and sugar. Put the top on the shaker and shake vigorously. Strain into a chilled Collins glass up to about 1 inch (2.5cm) from the top of the glass. Splash the soda on top so that it foams.

D'ANGELO VOODOO

by Drew Millard

The funk isn't something that you can just find under a rock or in your closet. You've got to open yourself up to the funk, let the funk come to you, flow through you, envelop you, become you. And that's something D'Angelo innately understands, perhaps more than any other musician of the past 30 years. Though he was already a known quantity by the time he and producer Questlove of the Roots set about to record *Voodoo*—his debut album *Brown Sugar* had gone platinum, after all—it's his second album that feels like a 79-minute trickle right up and out the geyser of pure, unadulterated funk.

While it might sound effortless when you listen to it, the recording of *Voodoo* was anything but. The product of nearly four years of jamming, experimentation, and pure trial and error by D and Questlove inside the legendary Electric Lady Studios in New York City, the album was an effort to capture the same sort of ineffable energy that ran through records like Prince's *Parade*, Sly & the Family Stone's *There's a Riot Goin' On*, and Funkadelic's *Maggot Brain*. Speaking to *Noisey* in 2014, Questlove said that many of the album's tracks began as meandering improvisatory recordings that would be analyzed, compressed, and re-recorded until they'd been whittled down to their most essential elements. As a result,

rarely does a track on *Voodoo* end where it begins, instead seemingly following its own whimsical muse. Nearly every song eclipses the five-minute mark, but they never feel long—if anything, time seems to speed up while you're listening to this record. Its touchstones range from funk to soul to Afrobeat to psychedelia to soca to jazz, but describing *Voodoo* with mere words is a disservice to its ineffable nature. It demands your attention but is never difficult; it rewards analysis of its textures but never prioritizes process over product.

As perfect as *Voodoo* is, it was nearly D'Angelo's undoing. Echoing the album cover's simple yet powerful image, the music video for "Untitled (How Does It Feel)" is comprised of a now-iconic single shot of the shirtless, ripped D'Angelo, coyly seducing the viewer for upwards of seven minutes. That video turned the shy D'Angelo into a sex symbol, and his subsequent tour only reinforced that notion. Shell-shocked by his new public image, D'Angelo retreated from the spotlight, lapsing into depression and drug abuse, sporadically showing his face until fully re-emerging with 2014's incredible, out-of-nowhere comeback album, *Black Messiah*. But no matter what, *Voodoo* remains a singular, perfect document, a work of R&B magical realism for the ages.

Like this?
Check out these three too

**Erykah Badu
Baduizm**

**Maxwell
Maxwell's Urban
Hang Suite**

**Ready for
the World
Ready for
the World**

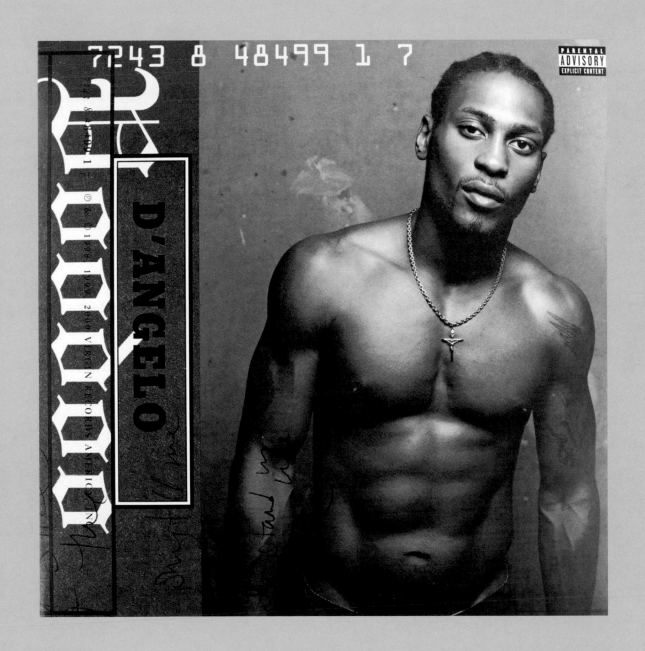

DAFT PUNK
RANDOM ACCESS MEMORIES

by Andrew Winistorfer

In which two French techno heroes return with their first new album in eight years, and instead of it being the harder, better, faster, stronger electro rock that everyone expected, it turned out they spent the years listening to '70s soft-rock records and paying the session players from those records to play on their album. *Random Access Memories* was destined to be a mega-hit regardless—the furor and appreciation of Daft Punk was never higher, thanks to the booming of EDM and the realization that *Discovery* was a classic—but you'd be hard-pressed to find a more unlikely hit album in 2013. The famous helmets appear as two halves fused into one on the album cover, and the pair's knack for drawing on others' sounds and fusing them with their own is never more on display than here: *Random Access Memories* draws from Al Jarreau, Chic, Steely Dan, the Doobie Brothers, and the Cars, and somehow that makes sense, because Daft Punk knew they could make whatever album they wanted without pressure.

Of course it helps that *Random Access Memories* came packaged with "Get Lucky," a song that single-handedly revived roller-rink anthems, Pharrell Williams's solo performing career, Nile Rodgers's producing/guitar-playing career, and, thanks to its video, sequined suit coats.

But that wasn't enough for Daft Punk; they also exhumed the career of forgotten "Rainbow Connection" singer-songwriter Paul Williams ("Touch"), gave house-legend Todd Edwards a second career option as the lead singer of a Steely Dan cover band ("Fragments of Time"), somehow turned one of the dudes from Animal Collective into a pop star ("Doin' It Right"), made the possibility of more solo material from the Strokes' Julian Casablancas a possible treat instead of a terror ("Instant Crush"), and brought Giorgio Moroder to a new audience of disco-niks ("Giorgio by Moroder"). Daft Punk's greatest strength as the party-starting robots they were earlier in their career is how they could curate and create the best jams from the hottest clubs. That they could do the same for making a modern yacht-rock album was as tough to believe in 2013 as it would have been in 2003.

Daft Punk—who were famously seated sans-helmets next to the helmeted people they paid to appear as them—cleaned up at the 2014 Grammys, with *Random Access Memories* winning Album of the Year, and "Get Lucky" winning Record of the Year, among other awards. It was a rare occasion: the Grammys legitimately awarded the best album their top award. Hardly happened before; hasn't happened since.

Like this?
Check out these three too

Chic
Risqué

Boz Scaggs
Silk Degrees

Paul Williams
Just an Old Fashioned Love Song

MILES DAVIS
BITCHES BREW

by Andy O'Connor

Bitches Brew is one of those records that completely reimagined what we could do with music, and we're all still trying to catch up. Miles Davis found the common ground between jazz and rock; seeking to make a link between jazz's spiritual heights and rock's then-prominence as protest music, fused them in order to get every last bit of power he could out of them. Just before this, he put out *In a Silent Way*, the calmer precedent before the absolute storm of *Brew*, a revolution in and of itself that still couldn't force listeners to anticipate where Miles would go next. The Afrocentric, surrealistic cover image by Mati Klarwein reflects the heady, multi-strand futuristic complexity of Miles's explosive work.

His trumpet is more rapid-fire and harsh; those obtrusive squalls in the title track still hang on long after they're finished. They sound welcoming to those in with the changes, and the ultimate piss-off to the fogies who couldn't hang and just wanted "My Funny Valentine" again. John McLaughlin builds quite a bit of the bridge Miles is overseeing, with rock aggression that knows how to lie back. Miles believed in him so much there's a whole track named after him.

Electric pianists Joe Zawinul and Chick Corea largely drive the tense melodies that make *Brew* an uncomfortable but rewarding experience. The album becomes more tumultuous as it goes, everyone breaking under and totally loyal to Miles's will to change music

as we know it. It's almost danceable in parts, if you're into nervous shuffling and trying to keep up with McLaughlin's frantic lines, and the battling, yet somehow still cool, electric piano, with a drill-sergeant trumpet that isn't always heard, but is always there. In *Brew*, Miles beat the hippies in making music that makes you contemplate advancing yourself; he already beat them when they were kids who might have bopped to *Kind of Blue*.

Brew came just a few years before Miles's break in 1975, but what a fruitful period it was. The record soon gave way to *Jack Johnson*'s uncompromising vision of black rock and the avant-funk of *On the Corner*, not to mention two of the few live records (by anyone) worth your time, *Pangaea* and *Agharta*. It launched the careers of quite a few of its session players: Corea went on to form fusion superstars Return to Forever; McLaughlin later formed Mahavishnu Orchestra, the closest thing to true successors of Miles's fusion vision; saxophonist Wayne Shorter and Zawinul found success with Weather Report, and Jack DeJohnette is now one of jazz's most respected and influential drummers. Most importantly, it secured Miles's legacy as a visionary, as someone who doesn't know what "compromise" is. We're still so tripped up in trying to mash genres together that few of us know how to capture spirits rather than just sounds, and none of us will understand that like Miles did.

Like this?
Check out these three too

Roy Ayers
Everybody Loves the Sunshine

Herbie Hancock
Mwandishi

Mahavishnu Orchestra
Birds of Fire

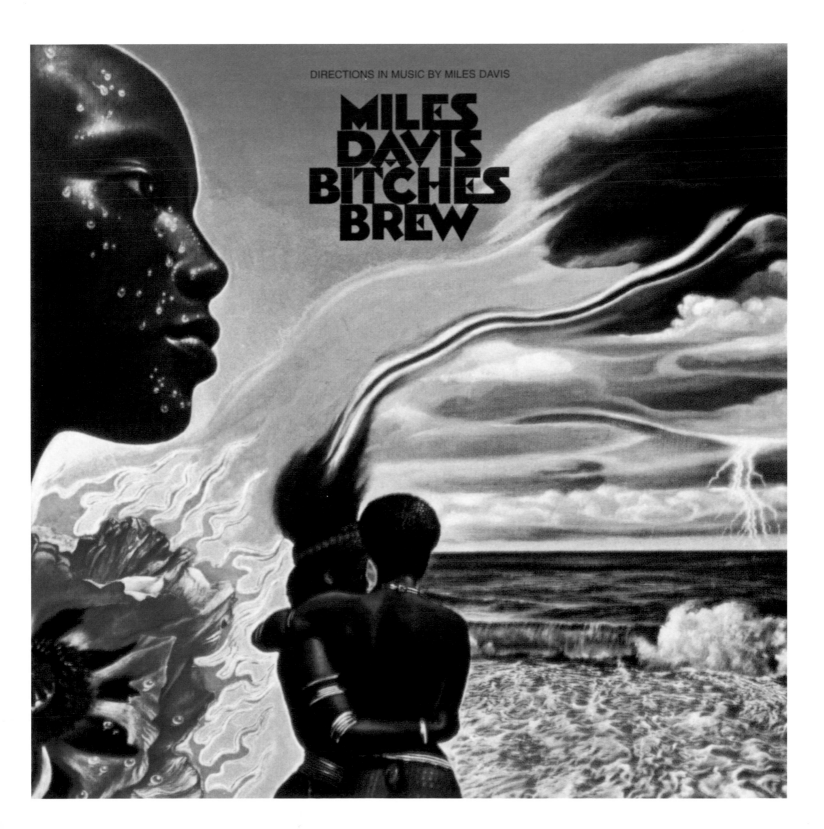

DIRECTIONS IN MUSIC BY MILES DAVIS

MILES DAVIS BITCHES BREW

DEF LEPPARD
HYSTERIA

by Ben Munson

Def Leppard's entire existence was once boiled down to a simple joke: what has nine arms and sucks? It's a sophisticated witticism that is only correct on one count: drummer Rick Allen did lose an arm after flipping his Corvette on New Year's Eve 1984. But the joke fails to consider how the band encouraged Allen to keep performing with them after the accident, how singer Joe Elliott helped with building the electronic drum kit Allen would play from then on, and how emotional it was when Allen made his triumphant return to the stage with Def Leppard in 1986.

All of Allen's struggles—along with god-like producer Robert "Mutt" Lange needing to take a break, the band scrapping the first 16 months of recordings, and Elliott catching the mumps—unfolded in the four years between Def Leppard releasing *Pyromania* and *Hysteria*. But whatever misfortunes befell the carefree lads of snug-fitting Union Jack shorts, they overcame and roared back with a full-length album that kicks off with a song about doing it. Despite its distinctly metal cover artwork, this is a work of out-and-out rock.

"Women" is likely the least recognized song stateside, from the devastating side A of *Hysteria*—every other song on that half was a huge single in the US—but it's hardly the only song about sex. Arguably, every song on *Hysteria* is about sex or how it bites when you're not having sex.

But if a Def Leppard song is only a vessel designed to carry a pro-boning message, at least it's impeccably crafted. The team of Elliott, Lange, Phil Collen, Rick Savage, and the late Steve Clark assembled pop songs so well constructed that even "Pour Some Sugar on Me" holds up after the billionth listen. But the painstaking production and absurdly proficient bridge-building is nowhere near as slick as on "Animal." Other tracks like "Rocket" and "Gods of War" offer more by way of showy studio effects, but "Animal" is shimmering and streamlined, effortlessly sliding in and out of the deceptively clever chorus.

"Animal," like every song on *Hysteria*, contains a crazy amount of moving parts that had to be mixed by engineer Nigel Green, an incredible feat that earned him 155 nicknames in the liner notes. Green's work and the resulting shower of sobriquets only further serve to highlight the huge amounts of effort and attention to detail that went into this record.

Call Def Leppard's music hyper-produced butt rock. Call the band out for having an odd number of arms. But don't call into question their commitment to one another and to making records. And please don't say they suck.

Like this? Check out these three too

Bon Jovi
Slippery When Wet

Mötley Crüe
Shout at the Devil

Poison
Open Up and Say...Ahh!

DIRTY PROJECTORS
SWING LO MAGELLAN

by Levi J Sheppard and Joshua Lingenfelter

Sometimes the most complicated artists are at their best when they unfold their complexities in a more traditional way. When Dirty Projectors released *Swing Lo Magellan* in 2012, they did just that. By highlighting raw harmonies and singable melodies, while also stripping away the more tortured song structures of past albums, the band reinvented themselves and created a collection of songs unlike anything they had previously released. Recorded over the better part of a year at a cabin in upstate New York, David Longstreth and crew culled the album down from nearly 70 songs and beats, the fruits of which showcased the band at their most accessible.

In previous projects, particularly the *Mount Wittenberg Orca* EP and *Bitte Orca*, Dirty Projectors have used the backing vocalists as a percussive element, similar to the way contemporary electronic artists like Four Tet, Burial, or Caribou might manipulate the human voice into something useful in carrying the beat of the song. On *Swing Lo Magellan*, the group expands on this, relying heavily upon the voices of Amber Coffman and Haley Dekle to carry much of the emotional weight of the music and to create harmonies that could rival the best of '60s Motown, while Longstreth himself stretches an elastic falsetto over the refreshingly straightforward and relatable lyrics. Tracks like "Just from Chevron" nearly cause the listener to forget they are waiting for Longstreth to come in on the track at all, while songs like "Impregnable Question" and "Gun Has No Trigger" would sound hollow without the assistance of such talented supporting artists. Before the end, Coffman seizes her feature moment on the show-stealing track, "The Socialites," a solitary voice over an intense instrumental beat.

Feelings of spontaneity and only loosely controlled chaos are what make *Swing Lo Magellan* unique among the rest of the Dirty Projectors catalog, and the easiness here is a testament to the vision of Longstreth, who simply set out to write individual tracks rather than tie the band to any theme or structure for their sixth full-length LP. The looseness of the arrangements and the informality of the recording make the same point as the final track, "Irresponsible Tune," that spontaneity is more fulfilling than living up to any expectation.

Although meticulously constructed, *Swing Lo Magellan* sounds live, like the recording is taking place while all the neighbors are visiting—in fact the cover image shows a neighbor chatting to Longstreth and Coffman. This homespun image reflects the "snapshot" feeling of the album—it's no accident that the banter and side comments are left in to remind the listener that this music is about the moment, when the sound waves are still lingering in the room. This neatly draws listeners into the warm and welcoming atmosphere of the attic it was created in.

Like this?
Check out these three too

Grizzly Bear
Shields

Talking Heads
Speaking in Tongues

Neil Young
Harvest

DJ SHADOW
ENDTRODUCING.....

by Ben Munson

The only thing tougher than digging through endless hills of vinyl to find just the right sounds to sample is finding a bad word about DJ Shadow's *Endtroducing.....* His universally revered 1996 album set an unreachable benchmark for sample-based hip-hop and remains indelibly vital 20 years on.

Endtroducing....., as the name implies, was designed to be the final stop in a series of singles, including "Lost and Found (S.F.L.)" and "In/Flux," that Shadow, whose real name is Josh Davis, released for James Lavelle's UK-based record label Mo' Wax. But Shadow was really the only person who moved on from *Endtroducing.....* while the rest of the world has been busy ever since dissecting it, getting lost inside of its downbeat atmosphere, and wondering when Shadow would release another album that approached its brilliance.

In Doug Pray's 2001 documentary *Scratch*, the camera follows Shadow into a catacomb of vinyl stacks beneath a record store in San Francisco. Presiding over a "big pile of broken dreams," Shadow calls the experience humbling. It's that pathos that drove him to seek out obscure music to sample on *Endtroducing.....* in the hopes of giving it a second life and exposing it to a new audience—

and indeed the artwork could be seen as an homage to the art/act of digging in the crates that produced this standard-setting album.

In "Mutual Slump," Pugh Rogefeldt's "Love Love Love" is stripped of its structure and reduced to hollowed-out kick drums and rattling noise. In "Midnight in a Perfect World," David Axelrod's "The Human Abstract" sends piano strikes piercing through the dusty silence. In "Changeling," Tangerine Dream's "Invisible Limits" is stretched out like infinite waveforms. All across *Endtroducing.....* small pieces of jazz, funk, rap, and psychedelic rock run congruent with eerie sections of standup, horror movies, and acid-trip explanations of Zodiac signs to create an unsettling stay in a dark archive you'll never be compelled to leave.

Shadow did try to leave, but never quite made it out. No matter how excellent his follow-up work has been, he's never been able to shake the specter of *Endtroducing.....* Shadow and his masterpiece didn't end up broken dreams within the vast basement, as he predicted he eventually would with almost all other musicians. But he's forever connected to *Endtroducing.....* and the souls he resurrected to build his perfect record are always destined to peer out the window of his beautiful, haunted house.

Like this? Check out these three too

J Dilla
Donuts
(see pages 114–5)

Pete Rock
PeteStrumentals

RJD2
**Since We
Last Spoke**

THE DOOBIE BROTHERS
MINUTE BY MINUTE

by Andrew Winistorfer

Formed in 1970 when drummer John Hartman and lead singer Tom Johnston teamed up with a pair of guitar players in California, the Doobie Brothers spent most of their early years gigging for Hells Angels in the Santa Cruz Mountains, and recording albums that melded their early influences of '50s greaser rock, country music, and R&B. By 1978 that original group was virtually unrecognizable to the band that made the Doobies' defining career achievement, 1978's *Minute by Minute*.

An instant classic of the yacht-rock genre, *Minute by Minute* is the moment Michael McDonald—who joined the band in 1976 when the Doobies were under contract to deliver an album and Johnston quit the band due to a drug charge and an ulcer condition—took over the Doobies, and arguably their lifelong legacy, for good. An entire generation would be weaned on the Doobies as the band that made "What a Fool Believes," a stunning, wounded song about a guy thinking a relationship was more than it was. With synths and a beat that moves as locked-in as anything by Kraftwerk, McDonald goes from being a session player—he worked with Steely Dan and others—to being the man that sailed the first ship of yacht rock. Everything that came after—Loggins, Cross, Toto, later-period Steely Dan—was just aiming for second best.

The rest of *Minute by Minute* is nearly as much of a wonder as "What a Fool Believes." From the syncopated keys and crooning of "Here to Love You," to the chilled-out-to-the-max electro soft jazz of the title track, from the throwback rock of "Don't Stop to Watch the Wheels," to the church-choir bombast of "How Do the Fools Survive?," *Minute by Minute* peaks over and over again. There's a reason this album had near universal ownership in the American Midwest in 1979.

The Doobies would never again experience the success they had circa *Minute by Minute*—it topped Billboard for five weeks in 1979—and the band hardly made it through the recording process; the only remaining original member during the *Minute by Minute* tour was guitarist Patrick Simmons. They've since become a legacy act, touring the finer casinos and fairs of America, but their achievement on *Minute by Minute* can never be erased. It's so great Michael Jackson claimed in interviews that he sang uncredited (and uncorroborated) backing vocals on it.

Like this?
Check out these three too

Christopher Cross
Christopher Cross

The Eagles
The Long Run

Toto
Toto IV

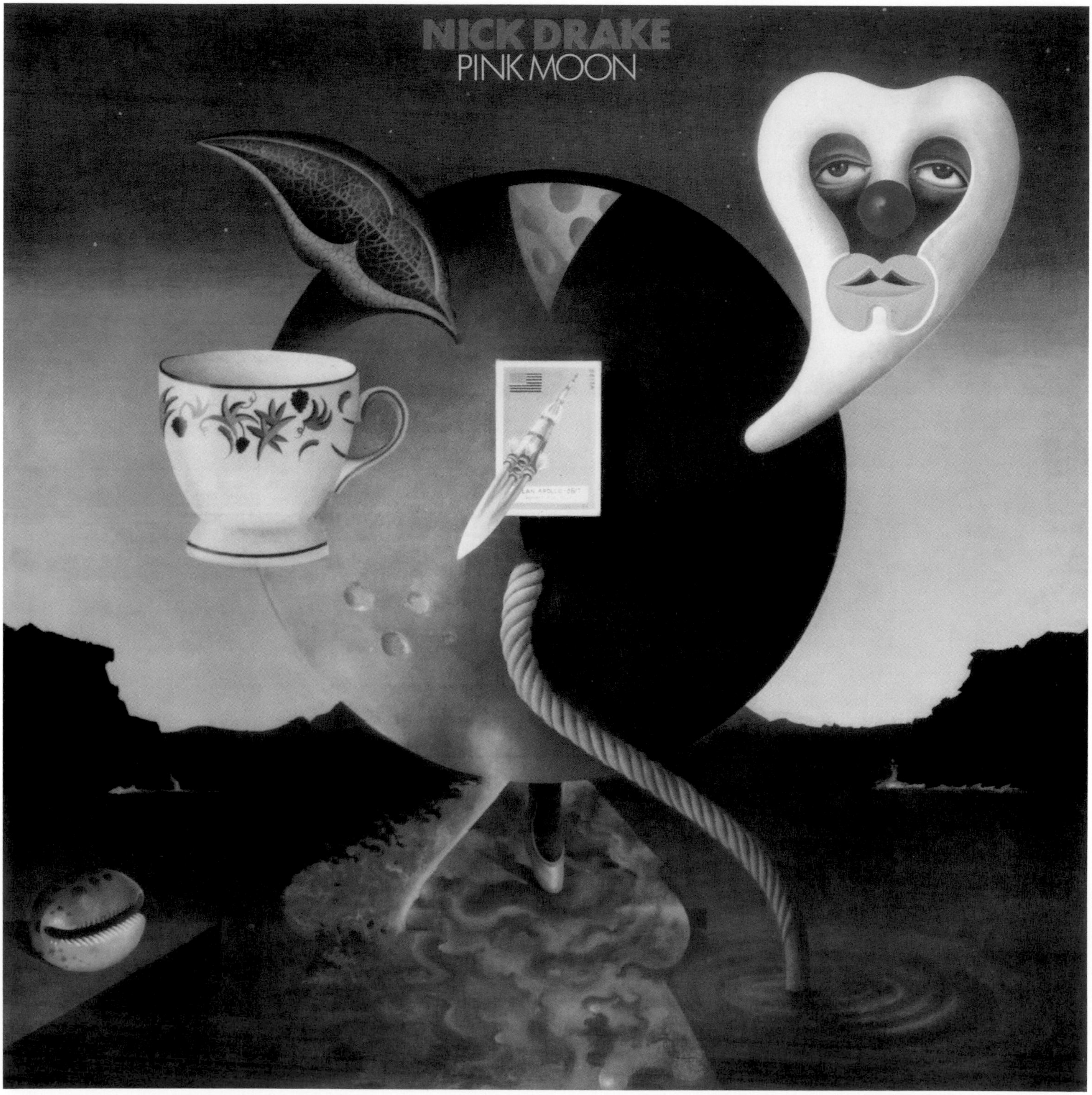
NICK DRAKE
PINK MOON

NICK DRAKE
PINK MOON

by Tom Breihan

When an artist dies, especially when he dies young and angelic and by his own hand, it can be tempting to hear his final work as some sort of epistle from beyond. You can do that with *Pink Moon*, the last of Nick Drake's three albums and the one that he recorded at 24, two years before he (probably intentionally) took enough antidepressants to kill himself. The clues are there, and the romanticism of Drake's early death is key, in some ways, to the legend of *Pink Moon*. But *Pink Moon* is too beautiful an album (aurally and, in its Surrealistic artwork by Michael Trevithick, visually) to give away its legacy to metaphysical rubbernecking. It deserves to be heard on its own merits, stripped of its morbid context.

What *Pink Moon* is is a spectral and spare and lovely singer–songwriter album, one of the simplest and purest and warmest ever made. Drake himself is the only musician on *Pink Moon*. He fingerpicks acoustic guitar in elliptical, complicated ways, opening up entire worlds through the ways his fingers play across those strings. He sings in a soft, inward sigh, his voice half-asleep and distracted. He plays a bit of piano on the title track. And that's it. When Drake recorded the album, he and producer John Wood were the only people in the room, and you can hear his fingers squeaking across his strings. Wood knew what he was doing, and the recording itself is crystalline and lush; this isn't a lo-fi 4-track type of deal. Still, it's a powerfully intimate piece of work; hearing it, you feel like you're alone in a room with Drake.

On the two albums he'd made before *Pink Moon*, Drake worked with sharp arrangers and studio musicians, making orchestral folk pop that never managed to turn him into a star. *Pink Moon* could've been a last shot at becoming something. Instead, it's all the increasingly withdrawn artist had left—a beautiful shrug. It's over in 28 minutes, but when you hear it in the right mental place, those 28 minutes leave a mark on you. Maybe *Pink Moon* was driven by Drake's depression, but there's nothing sad about its utter, self-evident beauty. Hearing it is a nourishing experience. It's too bad making it wasn't enough of one to keep Drake alive.

Like this?
Check out these three too

Chris Bell
I Am the Cosmos

Jackson C. Frank
Jackson C. Frank

Dave Van Ronk
Inside Dave Van Ronk

BOB DYLAN
BLONDE ON BLONDE

by Caitlin White

Ask anyone their favorite Bob Dylan album and you'll reliably get one answer: *Blonde on Blonde*. It's the unequivocal New York City album in his catalog—even though it was recorded in Nashville—and it began to usher in the all-important musical era of the late '60s with a song that tilts and whirls like a parade, all while touting the importance of marijuana. Then again, "Rainy Day Women #12 & 35" could just as easily be a reference to the biblical stoning of an adulteress, that's how porous and rich the lyrics on a Dylan record are.

Aside from the obvious prevalence of his harmonica, and the rich Southern-country undertones, *Blonde on Blonde* is a machine built around Dylan's words. The gut-wrenching ballad "I Want You" is the simplest declaration of love and need to pour from this writer's pen until he gets real gushy again in the '80s; "Visions of Johanna" and "Leopard-Skin Pill-Box Hat" each construct towering, marvelous images of very different women; "Just Like a Woman" is a cutting—if apt—ode to the beautiful unraveling that is a woman coming apart at the seams. These songs are gorgeous little melodies, but it's their lyrics that elevate them to puzzling, mythic entries into the songwriter's American canon.

It's on the album's epic-length labyrinths— "Stuck Inside of Mobile with the Memphis Blues Again," or later, on the album's closer, "Sad-Eyed Lady of the Lowlands"—that Dylan reveals his ideal scope; he's in it for the grand gesture, even if it's over the lowliest guitar line. Above the melody, his words are racing circles around the greatest poets of our time, warbled and garbled in his signature drawl. *Blonde on Blonde* won't help you crack Dylan's code, but it's the closest thing to a cipher we ever got. If there is any album in this book to listen to on original vinyl, it's this one. It's the least we can do—oh, aside from getting stoned* while listening.

*Contrary to popular opinion, photographer Jerry Schatzberg states that the blurry cover artwork was not a reference to getting high; it was simply the result of a freezing-cold shoot in New York that caused both Dylan and Schatzberg to shiver.

Like this?
Check out these three too

Joan Baez
Any Day Now

Kris Kristofferson
Jesus Was a Capricorn

Jerry Lee Lewis
A Taste of Country

E-L

BRIAN ENO DISCREET MUSIC

BRIAN ENO
DISCREET MUSIC

by Tyler Barstow

The first half of *Discreet Music* feels like an awakening, and in many ways, it was. This was Brian Eno's debut album released under his full name (and not just Eno) and his first concerted movement into the ambient oeuvre he would come to be known for. It may be true that ambient music is a sentence that never ends, and if so, Eno is its principal grammarian. He is its first sentience-obsessed architect. The first one to teach its buildings to build themselves, a concept the album's filter photograph cover tips its hat to.

This album is the earliest full manifestation of Eno's self-authoring ethos. Half of the album, after all, basically wrote itself. Eno was one of the pioneers of generative music, and composed the opening 30-minute track "Discreet Music" using a complex tape-looping system, which, once set in motion, manipulated the timbre of different, melodically compatible loops to create something that sounds much more ordained or intentional than it actually was. Think of it as the musical equivalent of perpetual motion, which gets more powerful over time.

And that's part of Eno's schtick: positioning the algorithm and the scaffolding not just as vehicle and support for art but as the art itself too. Blurring the lines between finished work and the progression that brought the finished work about. His mechanics and methodology explored on this album would continue to evolve into the central nervous system through which so much of his later work would live and move and have its being.

There's always been something vaguely Abrahamic about Eno. Something sort of wild-eyed and wilderness-ish. You get the impression from both his music and his demeanor that he sees things others can't and wanders places others won't. And it makes it hard to write anything about him that doesn't come off as kind of disconnected or missing the point, maybe in the same way that most of the pieces on David Lynch feel. So it seems more appropriate simply to say that we are far better off to be living during the time of the continual mystery that Eno is; to be able to keep albums like this one on our shelves indefinitely.

Like this? Check out these three too

Aphex Twin
Selected Ambient Works 85–92

The Orb
The Orb's Adventures Beyond the Ultraworld

Tangerine Dream
Phaedra

EVENINGS
YORE

by Tyler Barstow

There's a piece of me that will always be buried in Charlottesville, Virginia, and I think it was always going to be that way. I remember, as a freshman in college, catching a ride there for a party and afterward feeling like life was happening without me, which, in many ways, was true. I went to college in the middle of nowhere and rarely left my room. It wasn't the social stuff that struck me, though. There was a certain holiness to the place itself. A certain magnetism pulling me not so much toward the life I was supposed to want, which is how New York has always felt for me, as it was toward the kind of life I was meant for. It knew I wasn't a big-city kid a long time before I did.

I mention that because Evenings' debut *Yore* is, and will always be, one of the albums that best articulates the emotions of growing into my own skin during the times spent there over the years. Evenings' Nathan Broaddus is also from there, and samples like the one on "Softly We Go" are a literal hearkening to the sensation of the place. But this album is more transcendent, and less provincial, than simply being a postcard from a place many of you have never been. It's one of the rare albums that immediately feels both achingly personal and contemplatively detached, in the way that it might feel to film an out-of-body experience from the perspective of your disembodied self minus the ego-voyeuristic stuff.

This whole thing is a self-exploratory tour de force. A masterpiece born from Broaddus's patient strolls through his own psyche. An album like this isn't made overnight, and it takes time for it to find its way into the deeper sections of your mind. But it will, and you'll be glad it did. Every time I listen to this album I feel as if I finish it a little more awake and a little more in tune. Call it whatever you want, but it pulls you closer to what is capital-T True. It's not surprising that Jon Hopkins loves this record so much, and I think it's one of the most underrated records of 2013. You would do well to keep this one close.

Like this?
Check out these three too

Balam Acab
Wander/Wonder

Baths
Cerulean

Nosaj Thing
Home

Evenings
Yore

ROBERTA FLACK
KILLING ME SOFTLY

by Andrew Winistorfer

An entire generation of kids got introduced to Roberta Flack—nearly 20 years after she was a Grammy-winning artist—thanks to the Fugees. Well, specifically Lauryn Hill, who flipped Flack's "Killing Me Softly with His Song" into the Fugees' biggest hit; a song so big Wyclef Jean was able to run for president of Haiti off his fame from that (basically). Flack was able to re-release the song as a dance remix in '96 after the Fugees' version blew up, and it hit number one on the dance charts.

For better or worse, Roberta Flack's legacy in musical history is probably going to come down to that song, and maybe her duet with Donny Hathaway from 1978, "The Closer I Get to You." That's more than most people get, but those two songs can't reduce the power of Flack's career—for a stretch in the early '70s, she was the biggest-selling female singer—or ignore her deep catalog of perfect jazz-pop albums.

First Take is more jazz-oriented, and was legendarily recorded in 10 hours, and *Chapter Two* is the one you own if you're a completist, but the essential Flack record to own is *Killing Me Softly*, an album that lives up to the evergreen single it spawned (plus it has an impressive fold-out cover).

Like all of Flack's records, *Killing Me Softly* is built on her show-stopping, limitless voice and her Walden Pond–pristine arrangements. *Killing Me Softly* starts with the stunning title track, before hitting another early peak with "No Tears (in the End)," a spunky tell-off to a romantic partner, where Flack simultaneously issues a warning and worries about his ability to make her cry. "River" plays like what would have happened if Flack signed to Motown, and the album's closer, the nine-minute torch song "Suzanne," rolls and picks up steam, constantly building toward its conclusion.

Flack was nominated for Album of the Year for *Killing Me Softly*, losing to Stevie Wonder's *Innervisions*. But at the 1974 Grammys, she won Record of the Year for "Killing Me Softly with His Song," becoming the first (and only, till U2 won in 2001 and 2002) artist to win back-to-back Record of the Year Grammys (she won in 1973 for "The First Time Ever I Saw Your Face"). She might go down in recent memory for her link to the Fugees, but for a time, Roberta ruled music like no other. *Killing Me Softly* was her reign's greatest moment.

Like this? Check out these three too

Peabo Bryson
Quiet Storm

Minnie Riperton
Perfect Angel

Diana Ross
Lady Sings the Blues

FLEETWOOD MAC
RUMOURS

by Eric Sundermann

Is there a perfect record? Because if there is, it's Fleetwood Mac's *Rumours*, an album that has continually shaped new generations since it entered the world back in 1977. When *Rumours* was released, it became the fastest-selling album of all time—moving around 800,000 copies per week during its hype—and rightfully would go on to make Fleetwood Mac one of the biggest bands in the world. But what is so appealing about it? For starters, the stories surrounding the recording—which cost a million dollars and took almost a year to do out in California—are almost as good as the album itself. There's that famous *Rolling Stone* cover from the year the record released that features all the band lying in bed together, limbs intertwined, some under covers, others not, representing how they were fucking each other in different ways at different points in their career and during the recording process. And then they made a record about it.

Rumours is a classic not only for its voyeuristic qualities (even the album cover with its seductive elegance has an overt nod to this), with band members peeling back the curtain so we can see just how emotionally complicated their lives were, but also because of its incredibly catchy, radio-friendly American rock songs. It's an album that on its surface feels light and free—something chipper you can put on and feel like the sun is shining on your face—but that hides the nihilistic qualities of the lyrics. "Second Hand News," "Dreams," and "Never Going Back Again" are some of the happiest-sounding songs that have ever existed, and yet . . . *Rumours* bares all the charming foolishness of youth, and embraces the hedonistic qualities of the '70s that we've come to love: drugs, sex, and rock 'n' roll, baby. It's a cliché, but Fleetwood Mac is the original cliché.

Like this?
Check out these three too

The Eagles
Hotel California

Steve Miller Band
Fly Like an Eagle

Stevie Nicks
Bella Donna

ARETHA FRANKLIN
ARETHA NOW

by Jes Skolnik

The bulk of *Aretha Now* was recorded in just five days with the Muscle Shoals crew, who were flown to New York for the sessions (as they were feuding with that studio's management at the time) and who had worked with Aretha and music journalist-turned-record-executive Jerry Wexler on their previous efforts together. The follow-up to the enormously popular *Lady Soul, Aretha Now* also spawned enormous singles like the big powerful "Think," which was recorded the day Martin Luther King, Jr. was assassinated. Other hits include a tender and elegantly sensual version of Sam Cooke's "You Send Me" (after her established gospel beginnings, Franklin was inspired by Cooke to cross over into secular music), and a sublime and sparkly version of Burt Bacharach's "I Say a Little Prayer." Whitney Houston's mother, Cissy, and her Sweet Inspirations were the heavenly choir to Aretha's one-of-a-kind voice once again, and the Memphis Horns' dynamic performance was only aided by Arif Mardin's taut, punchy arrangements.

Mardin was Atlantic's house-label producer, and he, Wexler, and engineer Tom Dowd (all of whom worked on *Aretha Now*) were hugely influential in creating the urgent, emotional, yet cleanly polished pop-soul sound we now associate with Atlantic's stellar '60s and '70s R&B roster, which also included Ray Charles, Sam & Dave, Otis Redding, and Wilson Pickett. Critics were concerned that their attempts to replicate the magic the Atlantic sound team had achieved with Aretha on *Lady Soul* would lead to her songwriting career becoming static, but it's obvious in hindsight this wouldn't be a worry.

The Atlantic sound team's production chemistry is surely responsible for the efficiency of this recording*—can you imagine making most of a record as complex and energetic as this in five days?—but it is Aretha's limber voice in its prime that is still the centerpiece on *Aretha Now*, and her enormous popularity and talent can't be underplayed in its success. Her vocal flexibility and innate ear for interpretation here animate songs made popular by others, and her own songwriting and arranging talent shine on "Think," with its classic, goosebump-inducing gospel bridge ("Freedom! Freedom! Freedom!"), made even more urgent by its historical context.

*An underrated part of the Atlantic machinery was photographer David Gahr, who was a prolific photographer of blues and R&B artists of the era, and whose confidently mischevious photo of Aretha graces the cover here.

Like this?
Check out these three too

Etta James
At Last!

Nina Simone
I Put a Spell on You

The Supremes
Where Did Our Love Go?

SOUTHERN HARMONY

Ingredients

1¼ fl oz (40ml) Jack Daniel's
Tennessee whiskey

¾ fl oz (20ml) Southern Comfort
bourbon and peach liqueur

4 fl oz (125ml) sweet-and-sour mix

splash of lemon-lime soda

1 lemon wedge, to garnish

ice

Method

Half fill a sour glass with ice then pour over
the whiskey, peach liqueur, sweet-and-sour
mix, and soda. Stir, garnish with the lemon
wedge and serve.

FUNKADELIC
MAGGOT BRAIN

by Luke Winkie

The legend states that a zonked George Clinton told Eddie Hazel to play like his mother had just died. What followed was, without a doubt, the greatest guitar solo ever recorded. Ten minutes of aching, tender glory; arguably the most singular moment in the history of music. It will leave you altered; on your knees, begging for mercy, begging for more. It's hard to understand how something this devastating can even exist, but here it is, and things will never be the same.

However, you shouldn't let *Maggot Brain* fool you. Yes, the title track is mythic, indomitable, and very, very serious, but like most of the music that came from the Funkadelic–Parliament collective, this is still a very joyful album hiding beneath the epic dourness. "Can You Get to That" might be most famous for being the bedrock sample of Sleigh Bells' eternal "Rill Rill," but that rollicking acoustic guitar will always sound best underneath the pureness of Garry Shider and Ray Davis. Sure, it's still probably about death (we open with "I once had a life/Or maybe a life had me"), but the afterlife is bright, fun, and full of all the weirdness they've been looking for on planet earth.

A few short months after *Maggot Brain* was released in 1971, a huge chunk of Funkadelic's core lineup would leave. Rhythm guitarist Tawl Ross suffered a profoundly damaging acid trip and subsequently dropped out of the band, as did Hazel and Billy Nelson, who left over financial issues. This was the last time they were truly great, effortless, and cool. Thirty-four people have since been in and out of Funkadelic, and George Clinton owns a contemporary reputation about as tarnished as Sly Stone. But none of that matters, because *Maggot Brain*'s portal is still wide open, and welcoming new astronauts to this very day.

Like this?
Check out these three too

**Isaac Hayes
Hot Buttered
Soul**

**Parliament
Motor Booty
Affair**

**Sly and the
Family Stone
There's a
Riot Goin' On**

W-218

FUNKADELIC

MAGGOT BRAIN

WESTBOUND

PETER GABRIEL
PETER GABRIEL [3]

by Jes Skolnik

Fiercely political and artistically forward-thinking, *Peter Gabriel [3]* (known as *Melt* for its Hipgnosis cover art, taken with a Polaroid camera and manipulated as it developed) was the album that established Gabriel as a solo artist post-Genesis and as a studio innovator. (The album also raised the profile of producer Steve Lillywhite, who had previously worked on several notable new-wave and post-punk records, and would go on to produce U2 and other big-name rock acts.) Upon hearing the album for the first time, Atlantic Records A&R deemed it "too experimental" and dropped Gabriel from its roster; picked up again by Mercury Records, the album sped to the top of the UK charts.

Gabriel's successor in Genesis, Phil Collins, appears on drums on several tracks. Responding to Gabriel's request that Collins and fellow drummer Jerry Marotta not use cymbals at any point on the record, Lillywhite, Collins, Gabriel, and engineer Hugh Padgham experimented together to come up with a studio solution that would "punch up" the drum sound and make it more powerful in the absence of crashing cymbal punctuation. The gated-reverb technique they developed for the track "Intruder" would be the first recorded use of this sound, which would go on to be one of Collins's musical signatures in his '80s pop career (most notably on the stark "In the Air Tonight").

Besides Collins, there are a number of high-profile guests taking musical risks on *Peter Gabriel [3]*: Robert Fripp's (of King Crimson) bent, precarious guitar solo on "I Don't Remember"; Paul Weller's (of The Jam) aggressive guitar style on "And Through the Wire"; Kate Bush's ghostly vocals on "No Self Control"; and the haunting hit "Games Without Frontiers." Gabriel has always been as much a curator and developer for and of other artists as he is an artist himself, and his ear for what others can contribute to his work without losing any of their own autonomy and style is phenomenally displayed here.

"Games Without Frontiers" (about nuclear war and international affairs) and "Biko" (about murdered anti-apartheid activist Steve Biko) were both significant hits, especially in the UK, setting the precedent and tone for Gabriel's lifetime career of political activism and commentary.

Like this?
Check out these three too

David Bowie
Scary Monsters (And Super Creeps)

Kate Bush
Hounds of Love

Supertramp
Breakfast in America

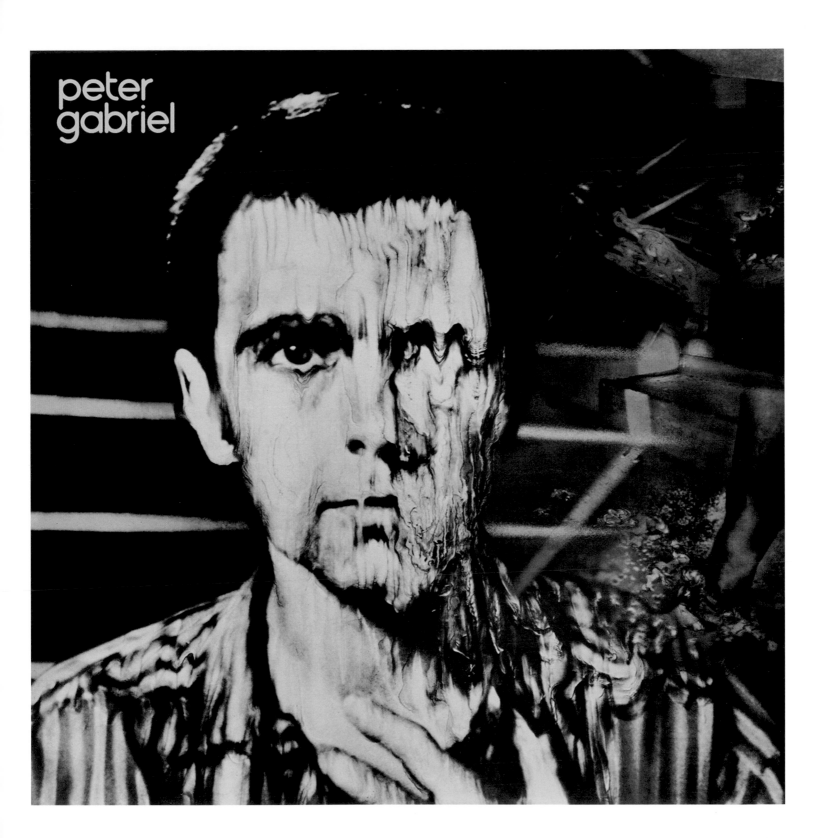

LION'S TAIL

Ingredients

2 fl oz (60ml) bourbon whiskey

½ fl oz (15ml) pimento dram

½ fl oz (15ml) fresh lime juice

1 teaspoon simple syrup

dash of Angostura bitters

ice

Method

Mix all the ingredients in a cocktail shaker half filled with ice. Shake vigorously and strain into a chilled cocktail glass.

MARVIN GAYE
HERE, MY DEAR

by Andrew Winistorfer

There are breakup albums, and then there is *Here, My Dear*. There is Marvin Gaye's storied, classics-filled catalog, and then there is *Here, My Dear*; by a wide margin the most-anti-commercial and left-field album he made in his 20-year career. But somehow, in the years since Gaye's death by his dad's gun in 1984, *Here, My Dear*'s stunning achievements became stronger, to the point where it's easy to recommend it as the essential Gaye album.

The story of *Here, My Dear* starts in 1975, when Gaye's second wife, Anna Gordy Gaye (also his boss Berry Gordy's sister), sued him for divorce. Marvin had a problem with spending all his money on everything the biggest R&B star in 1975 would spend his money on. Through some creative divorce lawyering, Marvin's lawyers convinced him and Anna to take a divorce deal that would give Anna at least half of the royalty money from Marvin's next album. In 1975, this would have been like winning the lottery; of course any Marvin Gaye album would make beaucoup bucks.

But then Marvin realized he had a lot of control over how much money his ex-wife would receive from the album. His original plan was to make an album that was "just OK," but he went another direction: he made an experimental R&B album heavy on organ sketches that detailed his divorce with all the gory details. He packed the album with slow burners filled with details from their broken marriage, like "Is That Enough," "Anna's Song," and "I Met a Little Girl." The most jovial track here is called "You Can Leave, But It's Going to Cost You." Marvin made the meanest breakup album of all time, knowing that Anna would be tied to its bottom line forever. The next time you think your favorite artist made a good breakup song, remember that Anna almost sued Marvin for this album because she had a good case for invasion of privacy.

There is no Weeknd or Frank Ocean, and no indie-rock bands claiming an "R&B influence" without *Here, My Dear*. Entire genres could be spawned from the instrumentals, and he somehow turns "she was too obsessive and jealous" into a singalong chorus here. It was the most poorly received Gaye album at the time of its release, but, now, its vindictive, expansive tendrils touch virtually all R&B.

The artwork of the album, the theme of which Gaye apparently specified to artist Michael Bryan, depicts Gaye in a toga in a neo-Roman setting, with an approximation of Rodin's *The Kiss* behind him—the back-cover image sees the statue going up in flames as the building collapses around it: an apt symbol of the ruins of Gaye's marriage that had inspired this remarkable album.

Like this?
Check out these three too

Dawn Richard
Blackheart

Bill Withers
+'Justments

Stevie Wonder
Innervisions

GENIUS/GZA
LIQUID SWORDS

by Gary Suarez

Picking one's favorite member of the Wu-Tang Clan is a volatile exercise, one prone to considered reassessments and protean bouts of self-doubt. First instincts may lead one to go with one's gut, only to find the selection quickly countered by a particular track, verse, or single lyric that sends the entire ranking into disarray and chaos. Even so, *Liquid Swords* makes it hard if not impossible to make a case against Gary Grice—aka Genius, aka GZA—as the superlative clansman.

Over the years, *Liquid Swords* transcended its cult status to become a landmark rap record, both for New York and the genre at large. Subsequent vinyl editions range from credible remasters to full-blown novelty packages replete with chessboard (it's not surprising to learn that the now iconic comic-book-style cover artwork came out of an intense, weed-fueled series of chess games between GZA and Masta Killa). More so than most rap albums of the period, it *sounds* like an album, and the start-to-finish listening experience proves that more than two decades later.

Two years after *Enter the Wu-Tang (36 Chambers)*, GZA's album emerged as its aesthetic and spiritual sequel. Sure, RZA crafted nearly all the beats behind a wave of solo efforts by Ghostface Killah, Method Man, Ol' Dirty Bastard, and Raekwon, but *Liquid Swords* best reprised both the Wu's martial-arts obsessions and dexterous lyricism. The analog warmth of the production comes as a direct consequence of the musical sample sources, curatorially culled from vaguely familiar records by the likes of jazzbo Cannonball Adderley, soft rockers Three Dog Night, and soul men The Dramatics, among others.

Beyond the respectful crate digging and liberal appropriation of monologues from grindhouse favorite *Shogun Assassin*, GZA's consummate microphone skills are what make *Liquid Swords* such an essential release, both within and outside the Wu canon. With a singular lyrical discipline, he demonstrates unambiguous parallels between samurai codes and street codes. His microphone turns deadly weapon, slaying fake emcees on "Living in the World Today" and "Shadowboxin'." On "Labels," GZA names and shames practically every then-active record label in the rap game—including the one that royally botched the release of his debut solo album under the Genius moniker—all in less than three measly minutes. The holistic support of his remaining Wu brethren over multiple tracks is valuable and even iconic at times, but it's their evident respect for his wordplay that makes this potentially ridiculous album of ninjas and wood-pushers so utterly real.

Like this?
Check out these three too

**Deltron
Deltron 3030**

**Ghostface Killah
Supreme
Clientele**

**Ol' Dirty Bastard
Return to
the 36
Chambers**

GUNS N' ROSES
APPETITE FOR DESTRUCTION

by Drew Millard

People like to point to Nirvana's *Nevermind* as the record that killed '80s hair metal, and that might be true. *Nevermind* signaled a sea change in rock's core values and aesthetics, a message that the everydude values of '80s indie and punk had won out over the folly and excess of bands like Poison and Mötley Crüe. Still, that never would have happened without Guns N' Roses' fantabulous fuck-you of a debut album, *Appetite for Destruction*, which managed to poison the hammy, glammy Sunset Strip scene from within by exposing its zonked-out, nodding underbelly.

GNR had already started acting like the biggest band in the world well before *Appetite* made it so. Though the band had its roots in the Los Angeles metal scene, they were never just a metal band. Their bassist Duff McKagan was a dyed-in-the-wool Seattle punk who'd been in the scene that would one day spawn Nirvana and Pearl Jam, and early on the Gunners were just as likely to share a bill with a hardcore outfit or the Red Hot Chili Peppers as they were to jam with Nikki Sixx. In their early days, they lived in a garage and sold drugs and robbed from their seemingly inexhaustible supply of groupies to get by. In interviews, Slash would say amazing things like, "I'm an alcoholic in the sense that I need to drink all the time," and claim that Mick Jagger "should have died . . . when he was still cool." At one point, the group were seriously considering calling themselves AIDS, after the disease they assumed they were going to contract from all fucking the same girls without condoms. As drummer Steven Adler once said, "We were like a gang . . . We play rock and roll music, and we will kick your ass." While the death skulls representing each band member on the album's ultimate artwork could be said to reflect that attitude, it's perhaps the more apocalyptic, hellish vision of the original that is a closer rendition, with a robot seemingly about to rape a woman just as a red metallic creature appears in turn about to swoop down and destroy it.

Listening to it today, *Appetite* feels like the last classic rock album, maybe the first grunge album, and definitely the most intricate punk-rock record ever. It was an immaculate combination of the Gunners' hard living, the edge of vintage punk, and the swagger of early Stones and Aerosmith. Though it's impossible to imagine *Appetite* without Adler's funky, almost disco-influenced drumming, or Slash's guitar work, which made technical virtuosity sound tough rather than the product of some Yngwie Malmsteen–style jackoff session, the record's heart, soul, and stadium-size ambition belongs to one William "Axl" Rose—an egomaniacal, crimson-maned Indiana transplant, whose interviews read like a Donald Trump stump speech, who told his fans to take business classes, and who let vile, homophobic remarks ooze out of one side of his mouth while proclaiming a love of George Michael and Queen out the other. Axl is a sensitive asshole who was full of contradictions, but you can't say he and the boys didn't give *Appetite for Destruction* anything less than their all. As Axl once told *Rolling Stone*, "Maybe *Appetite* will be the only good album we make, but it wasn't just a fluke."

Like this?
Check out these three too

Nirvana
Bleach

Ratt
Out of the Cellar

The Rolling Stones
Beggars Banquet

IGGY AND THE STOOGES RAW POWER

by Andy O'Connor

Raw Power or *Fun House*? That's a debate where there's technically no wrong answer, much like *Ride the Lightning* v.s. *Master of Puppets*. *Fun* is the "cooler" record, the more out-there, and one of the greatest. *Raw** edges it out because it is truth in fucking advertising; it is rock 'n' roll at its most optimal, music for the most visceral of physical experiences. It set the stage for punk to try and fail at being more feral, louder, more pissed than it. *Raw Power*'s only mission is to throw the wildest party in celebration of your total self-destruction— inviting you to play follow-my-lead with Iggy—lipsticked, semi-naked and smoldering on the cover photo—as your beautifully demonic leader.

It was their second chance after nearly imploding following an indifferent public and the fact that making *Fun* will destroy mere mortals. Iggy Pop took that chance to heart by delivering some of his lustiest, angriest vocals, blurring the line between civilized malcontent and pure animal. While Ron Asheton must have been pissed off to be demoted to bass, James Williamson was the man to sandpaper the good times out of '50s and '60s rock into volatile heat.

"Search & Destroy" is the obvious classic and most records don't have the fortitude to start with a song like that. Everyone's really been trying to top "Your Pretty Face is Going to Hell," and no one can get their hooks in you like Iggy could. He becomes Mick Jagger, if he bled speed, and Williamson is Keith Richards battling feedback and squalls. It's the meanest rock song ever. Elvis would have been executed in public if he'd unleashed anything like the *Power*'s title track—with the horniest, most impatient piano and Williamson's signature vamp with negative polish—on television. If Bill Haley and his Comets were actually on a comet heading to destroy the Earth, they would sound a lot like "Shake Appeal." Williamson's bounce is like throwing napalm at a sock hop. "Death Trip" was the Stooges' revenge on both the squares that could never hang and the counterculture that slept on them. Williamson beats a groove down over and over again, and when Iggy keeps yelling "SAVE ME," he actually might be talking about you. Iggy's only left standing because he's clearly not human, and had Williamson been on *Fun House* too, he might be jamming in heaven with the Asheton brothers. Play it loud, or don't play it at all.

*The original version was mixed by David Bowie, and since you can't libel the dead, I'm gonna recommend the Iggy Pop mix that's louder, ruder, and nastier. I realize I'm in the minority. Then again, I am an audio sadist who thinks Aerosmith may as well be Jimmy Buffett, and I probably won't be able to hear by the time this book is published.

Like this?
Check out these three too

The Damned Music for Pleasure

MC5 Kick Out the Jams

Metallica Ride the Lightning

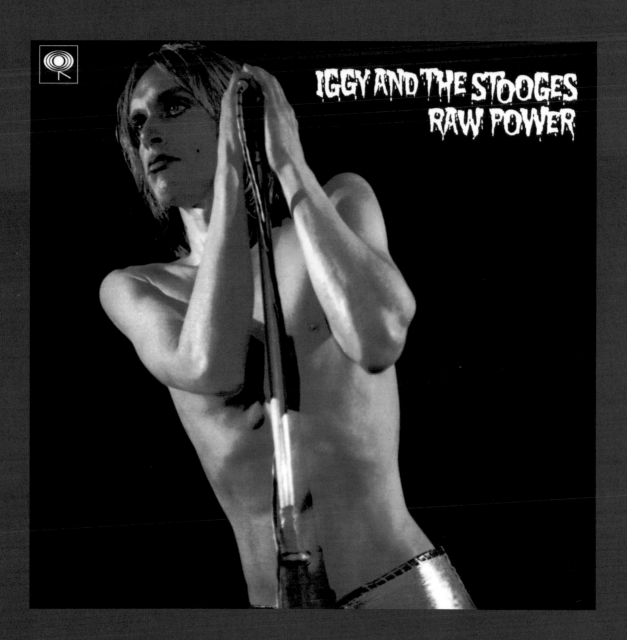

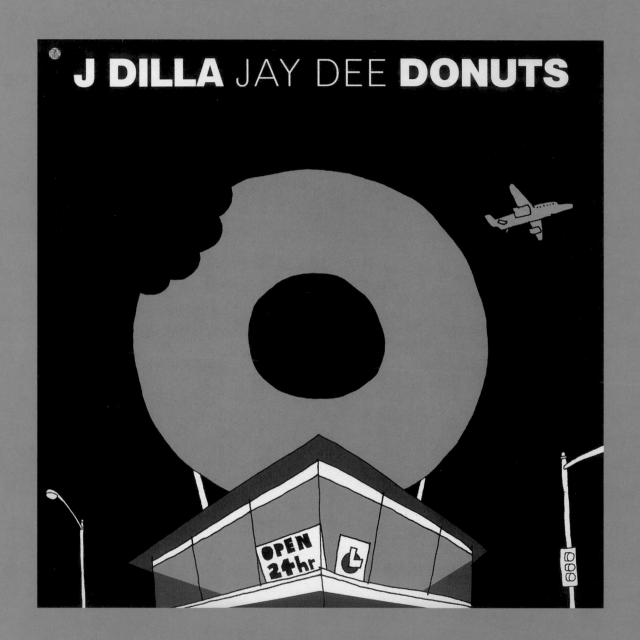

J DILLA
DONUTS

by Andrew Martin

Not many artists are afforded the "luxury" of a critically adored swan song, that typically being a final release before one calls it quits. But Detroit's James "J Dilla" Yancey was afforded that opportunity and embraced it while staring down death from his hospital bed. Among other talents, the world mostly knew the artist, also known as Jay Dee, for his beat-making pursuits.

You may have heard his sample—flipping instrumentals complemented on Common's "The Light," Erykah Badu's "Didn't Cha Know," or his remix of Janet Jackson's "Got 'til It's Gone." For all his top-tier placements, however, Dilla never slowed down. He was constantly throwing together beat CDs for prospective collaborations (some of which would later leak to the web).

Donuts's importance goes beyond its sheer artistic genius. The way Dilla chopped, flipped, and manipulated samples across its 31 tracks is astounding, as you'll pick up on new sounds with each listen. It'd be enough to get stopped in your tracks the first time you hear the blaring on "Gobstopper" or the emotion that bleeds through "Time: The Donut of the Heart." But like many other albums deemed "classics" by their fans, *Donuts* opened doors for so many different people.

Even the most unreceptive-to-hip-hop listeners can't front on Dilla's opus, often even going out of their way to purchase a copy (a rare feat for some). Much like the donut mounted on its now-iconic album cover, it's just too easy to love. *Donuts* is, in a way, a musical gateway drug for those listeners and, perhaps as a result, other artists. Without this album, who knows whether cats like Knxwledge and Whoarei would have credits on Kendrick Lamar's *To Pimp a Butterfly*. Would Soulection (the ever-growing collective of Dilla apostles) even be a thing? It's impossible to say, leaving one thing for certain: *Donuts*'s impact is truly immeasurable.

Like this? Check out these three too

Blue Sky Black Death
Noir

DJ Shadow
Endtroducing.....
(see pages 78–9)

Oh No
Dr. No's Oxperiment

MICHAEL JACKSON
BAD

by Michael Depland

How do you top *Thriller*? How do you possibly go bigger than the album that changed the way albums were promoted, won a record eight Grammy Awards, and would become the best-selling album of all time? That impossible question is the double barrel that stared down the newly crowned King of Pop, Michael Jackson. In the five-year layover from *Thriller*'s release to its eventual follow-up, Michael became the biggest star on the planet. Not just in the sense of a celebrity being popular in entertainment, but possibly the world's most-known human. Can you imagine that? How that would change a person?

Those five years were the lightning in the primordial soup that would spark the rest of his life. From then on, he would always be running from those years. The world came to know and dissect his now ubiquitous face (which came to shift many times over the years), and those years were the fissure between the Michael Jackson we knew and the Michael Jackson caricature that we would come to know. But the truth of *Thriller* is that almost half of it is disposable. Other than its thunderous opener, side A of *Thriller* limps to toss the baton to its otherworldly side B.

Bad was so important because it sought to address so many things. Of course, there was the obviously looming pressure to best *Thriller*, both critically and commercially—the title track "Bad" was originally to feature Prince in a duet, and other appearances with Whitney Houston,

Aretha Franklin, and Barbra Streisand also fell through. But it was important to Michael to make his first statement of who he was, now, with this massive audience in front of him.

That last bit is possibly the reason that this album resonates so strongly; it's unequivocally Michael's most honest album. Chronicling his rocket ship to uber-fame, *Bad* deals with alienation, paranoia, braggadocio, romance, introspection, and messiah complexes, and does so while being irresistibly danceable. The leather-clad posturing of the cover image signals the way for the title track, which, right out of the gate, is a hulking, macho opening salvo that seeks to affirm his seat on the throne. "Smooth Criminal," "Speed Demon," and "Dirty Diana" continue to push this edge with hard-rock flourishes, and closer "Leave Me Alone" was an angry lash-out at the tabloid culture that would haunt him until his last days.

But it wasn't all tough-guy bravado. "The Way You Make Me Feel," "Liberian Girl," and "I Just Can't Stop Loving You" all showed Michael's capacity to charm, and "Man in the Mirror" was his lovably schmaltzy attempt to piece together what to do with his newfound fame and power.

Bad is significant in that it's the album that probably defines Michael Jackson best. It's funky, cocky, defiant, paranoid, purposeful, sentimental, and, most of all, unforgettable. No other album captured the man better.

Like this?
Check out these three too

**Terence Trent D'Arby
Introducing the Hardline According to Terence Trent D'Arby**

**Prince
Purple Rain**

**Justin Timberlake
The Complete 20/20 Experience**

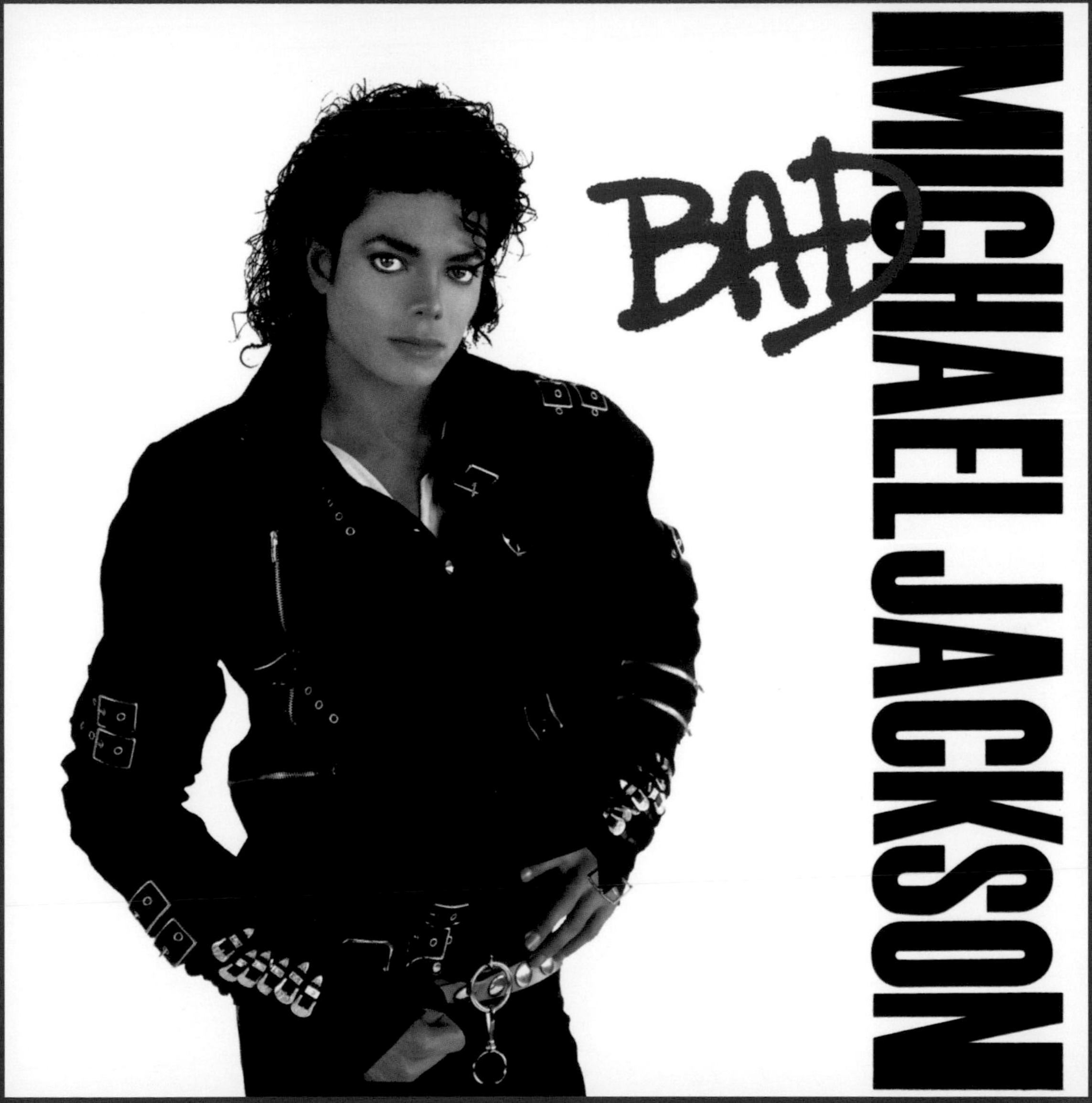
BAD
MICHAEL JACKSON

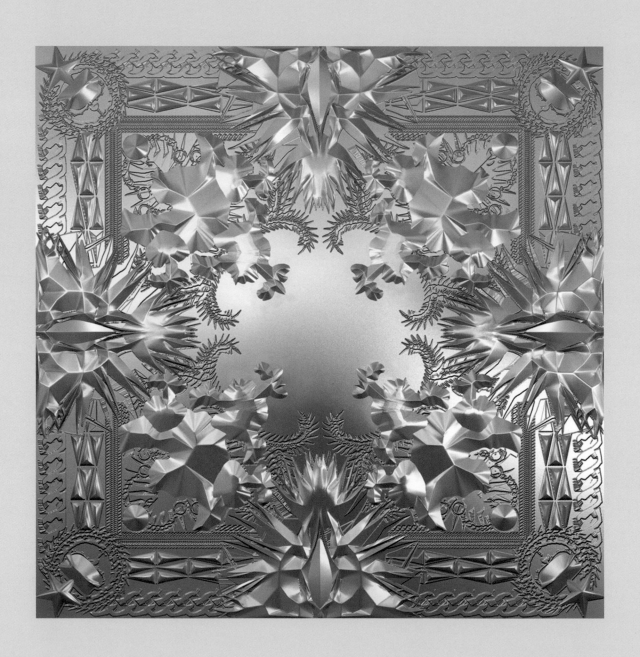

JAY Z AND KANYE WEST
WATCH THE THRONE

by Andrew Martin

At first glance, *Watch the Throne* is the epitome of gaudy, decadent hip-hop. Its artwork is golden and glossy, and its title is reminiscent of when Ron Burgundy cries out in *Anchorman*, "Hey everyone, come and see how good I look!" You feel as if you're simply listening to two musical monoliths continually brush their shoulders off while delivering nothing more than "luxury rap," a phrase Kanye West uses in his sharpest moment on lead single "Otis."

But *Watch the Throne* is far, far deeper than that. Look beyond the audacious "Lift Off," endless encores of "Ni**as in Paris" (they performed it 12 times in a row), and seemingly relentless bravado. Sure, Yeezy and Hov carved out moments to lyrically size up their contemporaries—those "talkin' real reckless"—but this is a record brimming with paranoia and insecurity.

Of course, that much becomes apparent if you truly listen to the damn thing and allow yourself to see beyond Hit-Boy's massive, career-creating "Paris" instrumental, and the boasting heard throughout "Otis." *Watch the Throne* beautifully illustrates the sleepless nights and harsh realities facing Kanye West and Jay Z, two obscenely wealthy and gifted artists who could have easily phoned this one in and called it a day. But they didn't.

Amid the perceived excess are constant struggles with personal and cultural demons; Jay delivers perhaps the most heartfelt moment of his career on "New Day," a sweet reprieve anchored by RZA's Nina Simone–sampling backdrop. The duo utilizes the five album-ending tracks to unleash feelings of angst, mistrust, and mental anguish, encapsulated by the following back-and-forth bars on "Why I Love You": "Got a pistol under my pillow (I've never been a deep sleeper)/P-p-p-paranoia (Cause the n**** that said he'll) blast for ya (is now) blastin' for ya."

The king-prince duo of Jay Z and Kanye West wasn't telling anyone to *Watch the Throne* as a conceit; they were reminding themselves (and others) to not let their guards down. They were also revealing how it feels to become a rich and successful black man in America who wants to pass that wealth down to his offspring.

Like this?
Check out these three too

Jay Z
Vol. 3... Life and Times of S. Carter

Mos Def
Black on Both Sides

Kanye West
My Beautiful Dark Twisted Fantasy

ELTON JOHN
TUMBLEWEED CONNECTION

by Zach Swiecki

Elton John has, or at least had, an unprecedented ability to craft hits. For part of 1970, however, John was just another musician trying to make it in the business. He would gain international success with his self-titled second album thanks to the hit single "Your Song," a tune that will probably play at every wedding ever. But before that album had even hit stores, Elton John and his longtime lyricist, Bernie Taupin, were hard at work on its follow-up, *Tumbleweed Connection*. Listening to that album today, one gets the sense that these two guys did not know how big they were going to get. Because you can't imagine they'd have planned to make a country-rock album knowing John was going to be one of the biggest pop stars in the world by the time it came out.

At the time, Elton and Bernie hadn't yet made it across the pond, so *Tumbleweed Connection* was a work crafted out of influence and imagination, not experience. The end result was a kind of psychedelic mash-up of the Old West and the Civil War–era South. Imagine an old-timey saloon with a shag rug on the floor and a lava lamp in the corner, and you'll begin to get the feel. It's an alternate universe, where Elton was the frontman for The Band (there's arguably an echo in the monotone cover of The Band's *Brown* album in the artwork for *Tumbleweed Connection*), making music that was just as strange, yet somehow more accessible.

The album starts with "Ballad of a Well-Known Gun," an account of an outlaw on the run whose jaunty piano and slick rhythm guitar set a tone that is rowdy and groovy all at once. From there, it's a slew of foot-stompers and slow-burners, some of which should not be listened to without a cold one and a box of tissues nearby. Highlights include "Country Comfort," a song that paints down-home life with such detail you'll wonder if Elton grew up closer to Birmingham, Alabama, than Birmingham, England; "Where to Now St. Peter?," whose dip into psychedelia puts everything by the Byrds after *Sweetheart of the Rodeo* to shame, and "My Father's Gun," a gospel-infused Civil War ballad that may make you question your sense of historical morality.

It might be surprising that the same guys who wrote "Rocket Man" could put together something like *Tumbleweed Connection*. But a close listen to their early records tells a different story. The twang in Elton's vocals, the characters in Bernie's lyrics, the occasional pedal steel in the production, all hint at roots in American musical styles—the cover image (despite its English location) gives a nod to Americana. On no other Elton John album will you hear these influences hang together more cohesively. And on no other Elton John album from that era will you hear such a distinctive lack of hits. On this one, he didn't need them.

Like this?
Check out these three too

The Byrds
Sweetheart of the Rodeo

The Eagles
Desperado

Rod Stewart
Never a Dull Moment

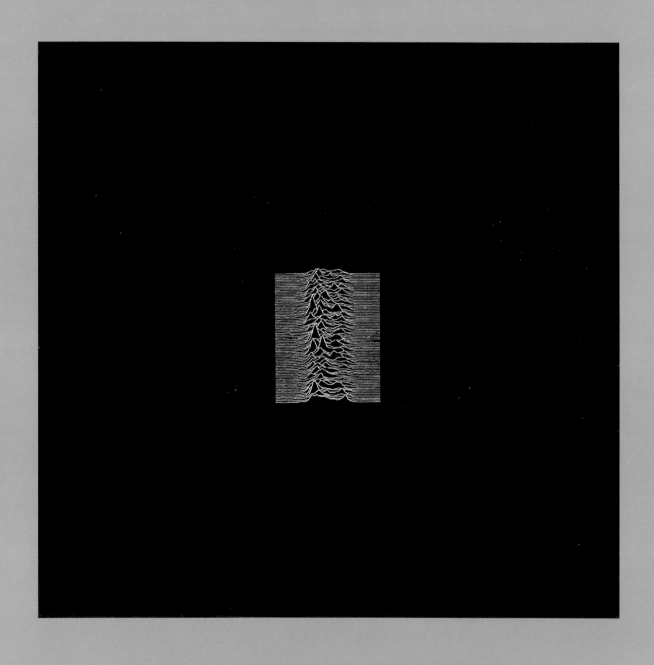

JOY DIVISION
UNKNOWN PLEASURES

by Geoff Rickly

It's hard to imagine a world where Joy Division isn't the stock answer to, "What does your band sound like?" and the cover of their debut album, *Unknown Pleasures*, isn't parodied on every other shirt at Urban Outfitters. But in 1979, punk was a cartoonish new trend, and there was no such thing as goth or post-punk.

Even if you can't imagine such a time, when you put on Joy Division's *Unknown Pleasures* and play the first song, "Disorder," you can still hear the sound of music changing forever. The sound is singular but every instrument in the mix is distinct: they are playing the same song at the same time but each member plays alone; every part is highly figurative, each representing different dimensions of postmodern life.

Producer Martin Hannett doesn't just capture the militant march of Stephen Morris's drums, he captures the atmosphere of war in the hollow echo of every hit: you can see soldiers' breath in the space between each snare drum; the blood freezing in the snow almost as cold as the look in Ian Curtis's eyes. Peter Hook's bass (playing an octave higher than traditional bass players) becomes the conscience of the music, alone in the war, alone in the busy streets, alone on the factory line; it wanders like a thought, equal parts hope and mourning. Bernard Sumner's guitars are all sharp angles and radio static. They represent the voices of others; the thoughts you can't tune out.

This is the world that Ian Curtis lived in. So when he sings, "I've been waiting for a guide to come and take me by the hand," he sounds like a lonely god, searching for a salvation only he can bring. His voice is deep and commanding, yet fragile, shot through with anxiety. It echoes, as if issued from the center of an empty factory. And the shadow of the factory never left Curtis's voice. For every prophetic line, delivered in an omniscient baritone, there's a later one Curtis delivers in a manic outburst, as on "Shadowplay," where he screams, "To the center of the city where all roads meet, waiting for you." These moments remind us that Curtis was all too human—he took his own life just a year after this seminal debut was released.

Despite the music's dark tone, Curtis returns repeatedly to a longing for connection, singing, "I tried to get to you," until it becomes an incantation on "Candidate." This may be the thing that separates them from the post-punk and goth groups that followed: Joy Division were disaffected outsiders looking for a way to connect, not entitled insiders trying to broadcast their disaffection and alienate people. So when Ian Curtis sings, "And she turned around and took me by the hand/And said I've lost control again," it calls back to "Disorder" and the guide he was searching for at the opening of the record. The tenderness of "took me by the hand" and the vulnerability of finding someone else willing to share the loss of control are what make this record so affecting. Knowing that Curtis would end his life just one year later, we hope that, for a moment, he was able to outrun that depression; we hope that maybe he found someone to join hands with and escape the long shadow of the factory.

Like this? Check out these three too

Interpol
Turn on the Bright Lights

Kitchens of Distinction
Love is Hell

Public Image Ltd
Metal Box

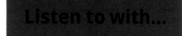

Listen to with...

DEATH AT DUSK

Ingredients

½ fl oz (15ml) crème de violette

5 fl oz (150ml) sparkling wine

¼ fl oz (10ml) absinthe

maraschino cherry, to garnish

Method

Pour the crème de violette and
wine into a champagne flute.
Float the absinthe on
top, and garnish with
a maraschino cherry.

KRAFTWERK
TRANS-EUROPE EXPRESS

by Drew Millard

Kraftwerk's *Trans-Europe Express* is one of those records you've already heard even if you haven't. It is, simply put, one of the primary colors of modern music. The chugging, charging three-song suite that is its title track, "Metal on Metal," and "Abzug" contain within them the foundations of modern hip-hop and techno, while the almost eerily pleasant "Europe Endless" contains within its gears the DNA for entire styles of synth pop.

The German krautrock scene was abnormally fertile with prodigiously skilled musicians. And as bands such as Can, Neu!, and Kraftwerk evolved within it, their musicians seemed to take a perverse pleasure in using their technical prowess to make the most minimalist, repetitive music possible. Meanwhile, the man machines of Kraftwerk had developed a fascination with machinery*: their 1974 album, *Autobahn*, had been an ode to Germany's highway system, and 1975's *Radio-Activity* explored both physical radios as well as radiation itself. *Trans-Europe Express*, in turn, was inspired by the train line of the same name, which promoted the idea of a united Europe—a priority for many Germans in the decades following World War II.

And as their preoccupations veered toward mechanics, the band became the first to embrace pop music's industrial revolution: *Trans-Europe Express* was one of the first records to incorporate sequencers in its recording, meaning that the band could program a keyboard line or drum pattern and loop it, letting it play until the band hit the other side of Europe. This gave *Trans-Europe Express* an even greater sense of rigidity than its predecessors, which in turn endeared it to America's nascent hip-hop and techno scenes. DJs could loop key passages from the record *ad infinitum*, allowing dancers to groove to completely seamless loops—a major priority in the days when breakdancing was king.

More than its influence, *Trans-Europe Express* is just a deliriously fun listen. It's the sound of four experimental musicians trying to make the most sophisticated pop they could while employing as few notes as possible. It was a challenge—one they excelled at with the precision and abject strangeness of men beamed straight from the future.

* This fascination is seen in their routine representation of themselves as not entirely human—on *Trans-Europe Express* they appear as posed male mannequins.

Like this?
Check out these three too

Faust
Faust IV

Neu!
Neu! 2

Gary Numan
The Pleasure Principle

CORPSE REVIVER 2

Ingredients

1 fl oz (30ml) gin

½ fl oz (15ml) Lillet

½ fl oz (15ml) Cointreau

½ fl oz (15ml) Pernod

¾ fl oz (20ml) fresh lemon juice

ice

Method

Shake all the ingredients
together with ice and strain into
a chilled cocktail glass.

LED ZEPPELIN III

by Andy O'Connor

III is the Zeppelin album you put on if you're looking to bask in your victory glory, fully nude, eating the most expensive cheese from Whole Foods next to your lover, rather than cause a fight because someone doesn't abide by that old time rock 'n' roll.

That may seem like an odd claim to lay on an album that begins with "Immigrant Song," where Jimmy Page's tumultuous rhythm speaks to the harshness of starting anew. Robert Plant spun what should be a downer rock anthem into a Viking conquest, which makes it stand apart from the rest of *III* even more. Most of the album is focused around Zeppelin's interest in folk, with acoustic tracks dominating. Zeppelin, along with Black Sabbath, were chief architects not only of metal's thundery bluster but also of its rampant darkness.

That's not to take away from "Since I've Been Loving You," one of Zeppelin's signature slow, bluesy burns. You've heard heavenly organs being used in the name of the devil before, but not in such a sweetly blasphemous fashion. Plant's praying for redemption to save himself—or does he want to go deeper? The way he sings, those screams of someone who relishes the pain—gets off on it even—it must be the latter. "Gallows Pole" is a traditional folk song from the perspective of someone about to be executed—without roaring guitars, it's still pretty metal. And you're gonna tell us that "Bron-Y-Aur Stomp," where John Bonham's thumps connect to our base lust for drums, isn't a real rocker because it's all acoustic? *I* and *II* are the rockers, *IV* is where everything really comes together, but *III* is significant because it shows the lighter side of Zeppelin's key balance. It's also worth noting that the Zacron-designed artwork—with its rotating volvelle revealing different images as it was moved around—marked the start of a more innovative approach to their packaging by the band, recognizing the need for design that reflected their own stature.

Like this?
Check out these three too

**Black Sabbath
Paranoid**

**Roy Harper
Lifemask**

**Howlin' Wolf
Moanin' in
the Moonlight**

LEE "SCRATCH" PERRY AND THE UPSETTERS
SUPER APE

by Jes Skolnik

Built behind the Perry family home in Kingston, Jamaica, the Black Ark studio wasn't exactly filled with shiny, new, state-of-the-art technology, but, within its walls, reggae producer Lee "Scratch" Perry produced some of the most unique, boundary-pushing, out-there sounds by experimenting with what he did have available. The imposing cover, with its rampaging, weed-smoking ape, both reflected the album's aural impact while simultaneously belying its darker undertones. Nothing at the time sounded like it—the murky, spooky, yet precisely timed overdubbed layers of sound effects and instrumentation Perry created with a basic 4-track recorder are as complex—perhaps more so—as anything recorded on a modern 24-track tape console.

Credited to Perry's studio band, The Upsetters, *Super Ape* is a startling, heady record. Perry, along with fellow producers Osbourne "King Tubby" Ruddock and Errol Thompson, helped pioneer dub reggae in the late '60s. Dub moved the focus of the music from the stage to the studio, remixing traditional reggae, stripping the vocals, pulling the rhythm section to the front, and adding back in heavy delay, reverb, and other effects,

as well as manipulated sound effects and snippets from the original vocals. Perry's work at Black Ark in the late '70s, including *Super Ape*, was a natural extension and deepening of these techniques.

There are a number of apocryphal tales swirling around Perry at this time—part mad scientist, part high priest, he reportedly sprayed his tapes with bodily fluids like blood and urine, blessing them with candles and incense, the dust of which would get into his machines, affecting the sound quality. (It's rumored he burned down Black Ark himself in 1979 to rid it of vampires.) *Super Ape* sounds, perhaps as a result, like deep, psychedelic mysticism. Bass and drum riddims threaten to swallow the entire production; vocals swirl, spit, and scatter, building a stairway to nowhere. The guitar on "Underground" is positively cavernous. "Dread Lion" moves stealthily, smoothly, almost glacially, snippets of haunting flute melodies flitting within like cranes over the grasslands. While it's easy to zone out and get lost in the looping echoes of Perry's world, it's these kinds of stunning details that make *Super Ape* such a marvel and worth returning to time and again.

Like this?
Check out these three too

King Tubby
Dub from the Roots

Scientist
Dub Landing

Peter Tosh
Bush Doctor

THE SUPER APE

Ingredients

¼ banana, sliced

2 fl oz (60ml) Appleton Estate rare-blend 12-year-old Jamaica rum

¼ fl oz (10ml) Del Maguey Chichicapa (or similar smoky mezcal)

¾ fl oz (20ml) lime juice

2 fl oz (60ml) fresh pineapple juice

¼ fl oz (10ml) Campari

crushed ice

Method

Muddle the banana in a mixing tin. Add the rum, mezcal, lime juice, pineapple juice, and some ice. Put the top on the shaker and shake vigorously. Double strain over crushed ice into a tiki mug or Collins glass. Float the Campari on top.

Notes

Original cocktail courtesy of Sean Kenyon, barman–proprietor of Williams & Graham in Denver, Colorado. Sean explained, "I listened to this whole album on my porch while sipping Appleton 12-year. Inspired by the entire recording, this cocktail has a little piece of each track. Silky smooth but edgy, and with a touch of smoke and a Campari float to represent 'Zion's Blood.'"

LORETTA LYNN
COAL MINER'S DAUGHTER

by Michael Depland

We're all better off for Loretta Lynn bravely striking out and leaving the small town of Butcher Hollow, Kentucky.

Coal Miner's Daughter was the introduction of country music to a lot of folks around the globe, and right from the opening lines of the record it's easy to see why you're immediately grabbed. "Well, I was born a coal miner's daughter/In a cabin on a hill in Butcher Holler/We were poor but we had love/That's the one thing daddy made sure of/He shoveled coal to make a poor man's dollar," Lynn sings right away. Maybe instead of a coal mine, it's working in a factory or cleaning hotels as a maid or bussing tables, but nearly everyone can relate to that. It's worth mentioning, the infectious honky-tonk melody it's laid over doesn't hurt either.

Though she may fool you by sounding so young here, Loretta had lived many a life by the time *Coal Miner's Daughter* was released in 1970—you'd be hard-pressed to find another country star from that era at her age dressing in what looks like a wedding dress on their album cover, like Lynn does here. A mother four times over by twenty and escaping deep poverty, she taught herself to play guitar, left her hometown, and hit the road with her beloved man, Doolittle, to play every honky-tonk she could find. She cut her teeth by covering songs by some of the greats like Ernest Tubb, Merle Haggard, and Hank Williams, but as she grew more successful, her self-penned singles are what began to start standing out. Records like "Fist City," "Wings Upon Your Horns," and later "The Pill" and "Rated X," would be banned from country radio (yet still go to the top of the charts) and cement her legacy as one of music's proudest muckrakers and badasses. Perhaps the most clever part about her songwriting was that she was never overtly political; she just told it like it was with her stories and let the listener be the judge.

And that was always the case with Loretta: whatever the tale, whoever was right or wrong, she had you listening. Whether it's about her upbringing, like on *Coal Miner's Daughter*'s title track, being cheated on and still loving someone on "What Makes Me Tick," or even being the mistress doing the cheating on "Any One, Any Worse, Any Where," she absolutely has you on her side. It's impossible to refuse Loretta's inviting, country warble as she tells us what's happening on her side of things. Once you start listening to her songs and relating to her in that intimate sense, there's no use. She's got you.

Like this?
Check out these three too

Dolly Parton
Just Because I'm a Woman

Ernest Tubb
Country Hit Time

Tammy Wynette
D-I-V-O-R-C-E

M-R

MADVILLAIN
MADVILLAINY

by Andrew Martin

Neither MF Doom nor Madlib will ever top their collaborative opus, *Madvillainy*. They don't need to. Yes, they have other fantastic releases in their respective discographies (particularly the latter under his blunted Quasimoto alter ego), but *Madvillainy* is without question their best work.

Upon its release in March of 2004, the album received mainstream attention like few (if any) other indie-rap releases before it. The *New Yorker* and *Entertainment Weekly* raving about a smoked-out, conceptual hip-hop album from two artists known for wearing masks* and favoring seclusion? Much like J Dilla's *Donuts* two years later, *Madvillainy* appealed to those who may have turned up their noses at rap music of any kind. Sure, it's weird, experimental, and offers no chorus for you to belt out in your car, but it's also lyrically dense ("Accordion" and "Figaro," for starters) and littered with some of the most ridiculous sample flips Madlib has laid to tape.

Beyond critical adoration, the album helped shape the brains of lauded lyricists Danny Brown, Earl Sweatshirt, and Mos Def, the last of whom's *The Ecstatic* reeks of *Madvillainy*'s weed-soaked odor (in the best way possible). For them, it demonstrated that you can find success in bucking trends and following your gut. That is, a gut filled with Heineken and whatever munchies you picked up at the nearby bodega.

Without *Madvillainy*, it's hard to say if we'd still be looking to Stones Throw Records for the next big thing to surprise. Or if we would have heard Kanye West rap over a Madlib beat in 2016 ("No More Parties in LA"). One thing's for certain, if you're going to listen to this album, be it for the first or the thousandth time, find it on vinyl. Madlib's penchant for flipping gritty, filthy samples into psychedelic-rap madness deserves it.

*In Eric Coleman's image of MF Doom, which graces Jeff Jank's cover design, it is Doom's challenging gaze that strikes you—rather than the indestructible-looking metal mask covering the rest of his face—reflecting Jank's aim to show, "a picture of this man, who happened to wear a mask for some reason, as opposed to a picture of a mask."

Like this? Check out these three too

Aesop Rock
Labor Days

El-P
Cancer 4 Cure

Quasimoto
The Unseen

MASSIVE ATTACK
MEZZANINE

by Gary Suarez

"Trip-hop" existed for lack of a better term. Like so much categorical shorthand, the catch-all provided an expedient way to describe the exciting hip-hop sounds coming out of the UK, particularly Bristol, during a brief window in the '90s. Eventually it narrowed to define a very specific style, by which point said style was already outdated.

It's easy to think of Massive Attack's *Mezzanine* as the exemplar of a short-lived genre, or, in more glib terms, as the theme-music source for the hit TV series *House*. Yet beyond these small facts lies an inopportune grander truth about this quintessential so-called trip-hop record. *Mezzanine* is one of the best rock albums, best rap albums, best electronic albums, best pop albums, and, hell, best overall albums of all time.

Trim back the descriptors and trappings of trip-hop and accept *Mezzanine* as its own thing. Musically, Robert "3D" Del Naja, Grant "Daddy G" Marshall, and Andrew "Mushroom" Vowles looked well outside the confines of the form they'd more or less defined seven years earlier with 1991's *Blue Lines*. The juxtaposition on the cover of a nightmarishly giant South American beetle (originally photographed by Nick Knight for the Natural History Museum, London) with the word "mezzanine" readies you for an album that throws together different sounds in a way that isn't always entirely comfortable, but is always riveting: Jamaican dub, American art rock, Mediterranean *tsifteteli*, and other disparate styles add up to a riveting set of songs, both somber and brooding. Del Naja's raspy flow never sounded quite as good prior to the claustrophobic, druggy jazz number "Risingson" and the sexually charged "Inertia Creeps."

The guest vocalists don't disappoint either. For her contributions, like "Black Milk" and the standout single "Teardrop," Elizabeth Fraser draws less from the ethereal enchantment of the Cocteau Twins and more from This Mortal Coil. Horace Andy's idiosyncratic tone haunts the slinky sleaze of "Angel," while Sara Jay's half-whispered delivery on "Dissolved Girl" distracts listeners from the imminent guitar chug that follows. Tailor-made for vinyl listening, album-closer "Exchange" comes with its own pre-loaded surface-noise crackle.

Like this?
Check out these three too

Air
Moon Safari

The Chemical Brothers
Exit Planet Dust

Portishead
Dummy

JONI MITCHELL BLUE

by Jes Skolnik

Confessional singer-songwriter folk pop existed before *Blue*, sure, but this stark, intense, vulnerable record established the gold standard, and few records in this cluttered genre since have been able to match its stunning balance of artistry and emotional truth. Written predominantly to cope with a devastating breakup with James Taylor, who appears on the album in several places (there are multiple personal allusions to their relationship scattered through the title track and "All I Want"), *Blue* was recorded at a time when Mitchell felt she had no energy or ability to keep up defenses for or against the outside world. Several decades later, *Blue*, and its stark cover, still telegraphs grief and desire so clearly as to be unsettling to listen to.

There's little filigree to be found here; Mitchell's voice and acoustic guitar speak in tandem, and plainly, through much of the record. "California" (a reflection on the fade and change of '60s ideals into '70s excess) and "Carey" are the two big full-band exceptions. "Carey," one of Mitchell's best-known songs, is a deeply personal ode to a friend made in a surprising place. Nursing a broken heart after breaking up with Graham Nash (of the Hollies, and Crosby, Stills, Nash and Young), her boyfriend prior to Taylor, Mitchell met American cook Cary Raditz in a Cretan restaurant. The two struck up a friendship, and Mitchell ended up living in a cave commune with Raditz and other hippies in Matala, Crete, for much of early 1970, and adventuring together. "Carey" was written as a birthday present for Raditz. Much later, recording the song for *Blue*, Mitchell channeled every sense-memory she had of her time in Crete in the studio to bring in all of the emotion of a complex, challenging friendship with Raditz. (Of note: Raditz also reappears in "California," as "the red, red rogue/He cooked good omelettes and stews." Mitchell has referred to the two songs as two chapters of the same story.)

Blue was recorded behind locked doors, and Mitchell has said that she would burst into tears if any intruder entered the recording sessions, so acute was her emotional tenderness during the recording sessions. It's rare that such bare honesty is channeled into music, and rarer still that it is as elegantly structured into the kind of memorable songs that appear on *Blue*.

Like this?
Check out these three too

**Joan Baez
In Concert**

**Leonard Cohen
Various
Positions**

**Laura Nyro
Eli and the
Thirteenth
Confession**

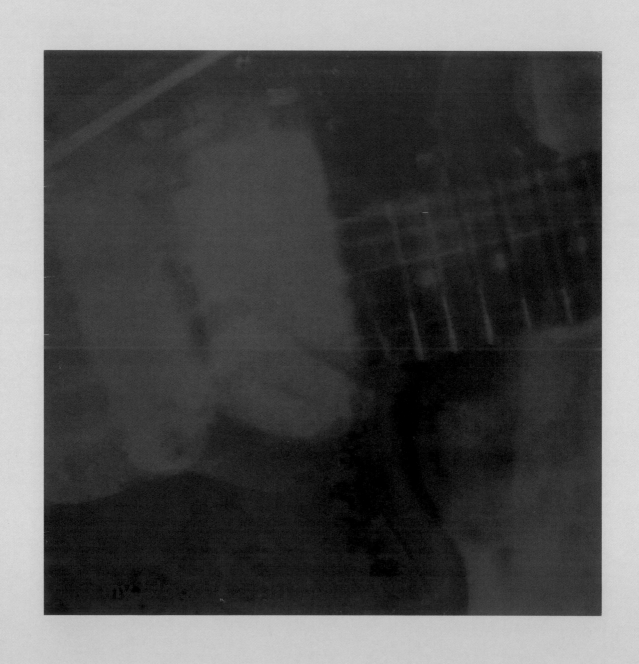

MY BLOODY VALENTINE LOVELESS

by Geoff Rickly

Twenty-five years on and My Bloody Valentine's *Loveless* still sounds like nothing else on this planet. Though its release marked a paradigm shift away from the sweet British twinkling of the Smiths et al, the paradigm never really caught up with MBV's shoegaze-defining masterwork.

Today you can hear the long, echoing arc of Kevin Shields's reverb pedals in every record from the fashionable guitar revivalists of DIIV to the black-metal revisionists, Deafheaven. Yet when the needle drops on "Only Shallow," there is no mistaking it: the metronomic snare drum, ushering in a wall of perfectly sculpted, deafeningly beautiful, singularly shaped noise that can only be My Bloody Valentine.

If *Loveless* is indeed a perfect album, "Only Shallow" serves as a perfect opener. It sets out all of the hallmarks of the record: wall-of-sound guitars, dreamy vocals, and hazy production, all part of songs that serve hooks up in the anthemic opening or unexpected pre-chorus. The fuzzy cover image is practically a visual rendering of this sound: a guitar subsumed by its own noise into a blur. Kevin Shields may be one of the most undervalued hook writers of our time: the high-flying guitars of the album opener; the call-and-response synths of "I Only Said." The fact that they're practically buried in noise makes them all the more sublime for being so notable. If other bands have failed to replicate the MBV sound, it's at least worth considering that a lack of songwriting chops betrays their ambitions.

Side two tumbles forth on the big waves of "Come In Alone." Bilinda Butcher takes the center spotlight, like a woman walking out of an ocean of guitars that churn in prismatic waves of echo, keyboards that glisten and tumble in the surf of noise, bass that drives with the steady fury of the tide, and a repeatedly steady drum fill that sits like a lifeboat, anchored just past the break of the waves. Legend has it that her famously weary voice on this record was the result of Kevin waking her up at different times of the night to record her vocals. Whatever the case may be, there's no denying that she is the human center of this otherworldly record. When she sings "Midnight wish, blow me a kiss, I'll blow one to you/Make like this, try to pretend it's true," on the Cocteau Twins update, "Blown a Wish," you forget you're listening to a classic record and just know you're listening to your favorite one.

Like this?
Check out these three too

The Jesus and Mary Chain
Psychocandy

Lush
Spooky

Slowdive
Souvlaki

WILLIE NELSON
STARDUST

by Drew Millard

As you let the classical guitars and easy organs of *Stardust*'s title cut wash over you, forget everything you know about Willie Nelson. No more Shotgun Willie, no more sad-outlaw balladeer, no hero of hippies and rednecks worldwide, no more country's answer to Snoop Dogg. At the time of its recording, *Stardust* was a fairly ballsy move: Willie's label was mortified when he turned the album in, damn near insisting he record another set of folksy, literary country-rock tunes instead of . . . well . . . what was this? Crafted in 10 days by Nelson and the soul legend Booker T. Jones (who just so happened to be Willie's upstairs neighbor in their Malibu apartment complex), *Stardust* reimagined Nelson as Tinseltown's tenor heir to Sinatra, belting out pop standards with the clear eyes and earnest appreciation for the material he was tackling.

Still, that's not to say that *Stardust* is a novelty album, or an essential listen, just because Willie Nelson was one of the first guys to turn left and record an album of pop standards. The record endures because of the singularity of its sound—a country wizard and soul master forming like Voltron to put their own spin on what Nelson once called "the ten best songs I've ever heard." The subtle push and pull of Nelson's Family band and Jones's Stax-bred soul-pop sensibilities is what truly drives the record, whether it's the undercurrent of disco thump that serves as the backbone of "Blue Skies," or the slide guitar rubbing up against the organs in "Unchained Melody," or Nelson's interpretation of "Georgia on My Mind" adding a dose of folk to Ray Charles's near-definitive orchestral-soul take on Hoagy Carmichael and Stuart Gorrell's original.

Yes, the record feels a bit music-that-only-people's-parents-should-listen-to, but that's less of a cause of this music and more of its effect. It's a testament to Nelson's unique vocal style—that expressive lilt, wistful when it needs to be wistful, bemused when it needs to be bemused—that *Stardust*, from its underneath-Big-Sky-country cover on down, feels so natural, like all Willie, Booker T., and the boys did was simply make real what had always existed in the ether.

Like this?
Check out these three too

Merle Haggard
Mama Tried

Waylon Jennings
Lonesome, On'ry and Mean

Harry Nilsson
A Little Touch of Schmilsson in the Night

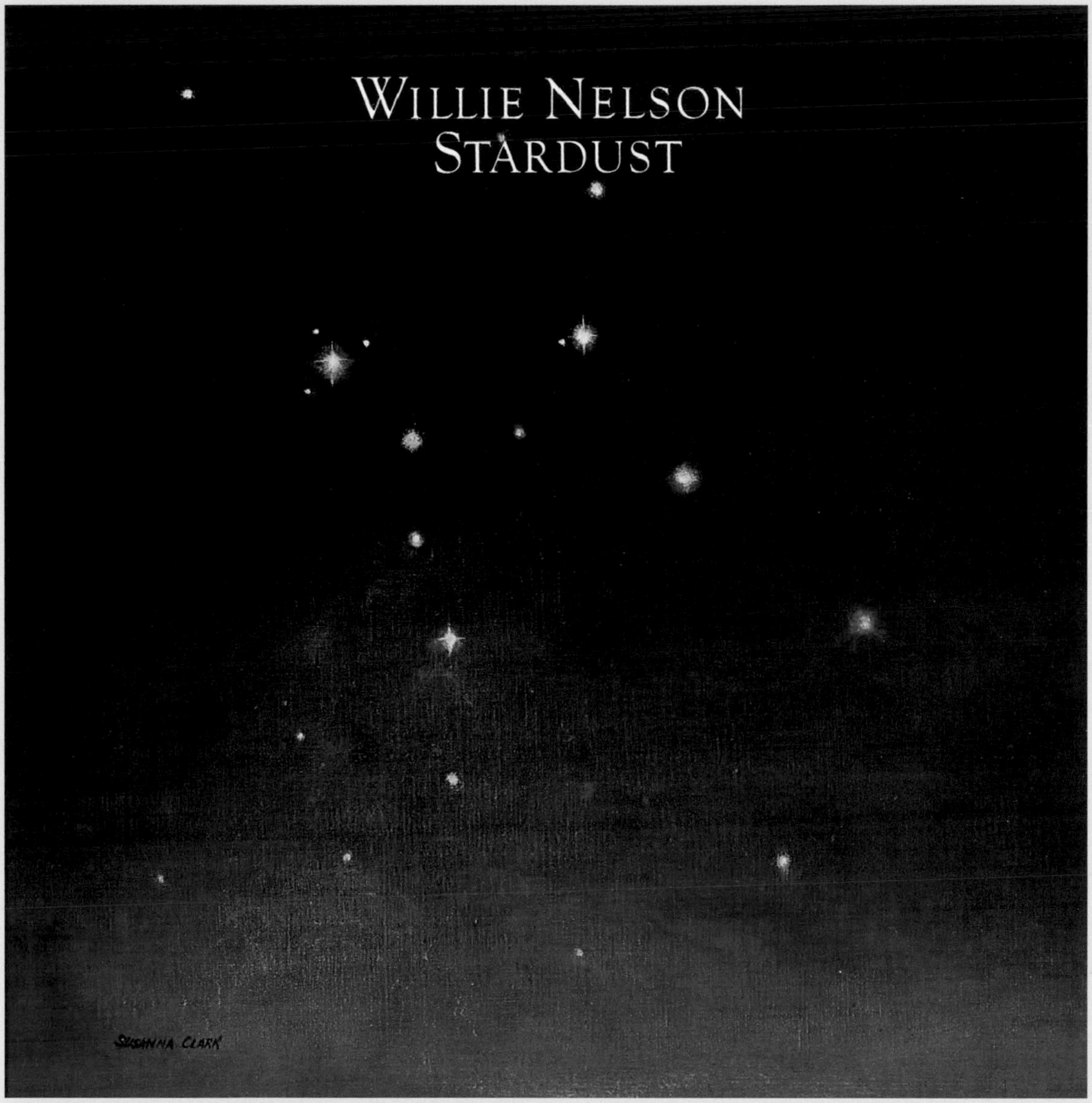
WILLIE NELSON
STARDUST
SUSANNA CLARK

NEUTRAL MILK HOTEL IN THE AEROPLANE OVER THE SEA

by Luke Winkie

Sometimes it's hard to remember that in the late '90s, Neutral Milk Hotel existed in real life. They went on tours, sold merch, did interviews; Jeff Mangum was just a weirdo lifer from Louisiana with an unsubtle crush on rinky-dink, pre-war Americana. It's hard to build a massive shadow when you're standing on coffee-shop stages. *In the Aeroplane Over the Sea* received workmanlike treatment from critics—a standard 3/5 from *Rolling Stone*, an enthused 8.7 from *Pitchfork*—and that was it. An album by a band.

But then, after the band's abrupt, mysterious breakup in 1999, something strange began to happen. *In the Aeroplane Over the Sea* became legendary. A new generation, kids without the humanizing memories of witnessing Neutral Milk Hotel in person, pored over its mysterious crevices. The surreal, unsettling, ambiguous album cover, the dying embers of "Two-Headed Boy Part 2," the chaos of "Holland, 1945," the delicious puzzle of what drove Mangum away from the music business and into hermitism. *In the Aeroplane Over the Sea* emerged as the 21st century's very own *Pet Sounds*, earning ringing endorsements from Win Butler and Jesse Lacey, and remaining completely remote from any reunions, archives, rumors, or paper trails.

There was a small sense of closure in 2012, as Jeff Mangum returned from the darkness to play a small tour of Neutral Milk Hotel songs for his patient cult. It was strange hearing these visceral songs return home. Again, just an album by a band. But I think we all prefer to remember *Aeroplane* as something outside of time. A bizarre, terrifying wonderland of singing saw and hurdy-gurdy, impossibly beautiful words about eyes, and sleep, and love, happily unaware of the lineage of everything else happening in 1998. It's an album on the edge of a universe, more questions than answers; nobody will ever be completely satisfied. And that's why we love it.

Like this? Check out these three too

The Mountain Goats Tallahassee

Sufjan Stevens The Age of Adz

The Unicorns Who Will Cut Our Hair When We're Gone?

JOANNA NEWSOM
YS

by Jes Skolnik

Even the most traditional folk music aims for some kinds of universal truths about the human heart and human experiences; after all, it is the music of the people. While Joanna Newsom is as unconventional as a folkie comes—as the Benjamin Vierling artwork of her as a Druid priestess adorning the cover testifies—that universal heart is her main concern, and she gets to it directly, beautifully, and uniquely on *Ys*, her second album.

Ys is Newsom encoding the prior year of her life to making the record into fantastical myth; it is named for an imaginary city from Newsom's dreams that supposedly existed out of time on the coast of Brittany. The five lengthy tracks on the album center Newsom and her harp and piano among full orchestral arrangements by Newsom herself with legendary cinematic composer, Beach Boys collaborator and art-pop originator Van Dyke Parks. Newsom has said that she was inspired by Parks's 1968 *Song Cycle* album, which reframed traditional and classical composition in '60s pop terms, and British folk-rocker Roy Harper's 1971 masterpiece *Stormcock* (upon which Led Zeppelin's Jimmy Page appears,

uncredited) to create the sonic world of *Ys*, which similarly mixes traditional folk with indie pop and baroque flourishes. The album was recorded (by Steve Albini) and mixed (by Jim O'Rourke) with all analog equipment.

The epic structures and arrangements of *Ys*, as intricate and complicated as the fabled Unicorn Tapestries, highlight rather than obscure the intimate lyrical content, which mostly swirls around grief and turmoil. Newsom had experienced chronic illness, was in the midst of a volatile ending to her relationship with her longtime then-boyfriend Bill Callahan (Smog), who does make a guest appearance, and was dealing with the sudden death of a dear friend ("Cosmia" is the elegy here). The delicate, direct "Emily," named for and addressed to her younger sister, who sings backup vocals on the recorded version, is part tribute and part open letter. Yet, despite their vulnerable and immediate content, these songs seem just as dreamed-to-life as they do intentionally created. Newsom is her own fabled character here, but she allows the music to lead her journey rather than soundtracking music to a predetermined narrative.

Like this?
Check out these three too

Devendra Banhart Cripple Crow

Roy Harper Stormcock

Marissa Nadler Little Hells

 UNPLUGGED
IN NEW YORK

NIRVANA
MTV UNPLUGGED
IN NEW YORK

by Tom Breihan

For those of us who came of pop-music age around the time *Nevermind* blew up, Nirvana's legacy has nothing to do with the annihilation of hair metal or the rise of grunge or the sudden popularity of flannel. Instead, their legacy was this: we'd never seen musicians existing on such a grand level and bringing a deep sense of sincerity to everything they did. Kurt Cobain could do the things that other rock stars did. He could tour arenas, appear on magazine covers, and tape an episode of *MTV Unplugged*, but he would do it while seeming tragically, vulnerably human—something that even a close contemporary like Michael Stipe never quite achieved.

Nirvana recorded their *Unplugged* episode about five months before Cobain took his own life. It's a personal performance, a document of a wounded soul, but it's also an example of a band that knew exactly what it was doing. *Unplugged* was a commercial juggernaut by 1993, and people like Eric Clapton and Mariah Carey had landed some of their biggest hits by doing coffee-shop renditions of their own songs for MTV's cameras. On a certain level, that's what Nirvana did too. They played the

hits ("Come as You Are," "All Apologies") and the beloved album tracks ("About a Girl," "Dumb"). They were playing the game.

But Cobain also took the opportunity to put his audience up on underground sounds, playing songs from the Vaselines and the Meat Puppets with the same conviction that he used for his own music. He turned David Bowie's "The Man Who Sold the World" into a sadder, more open-hearted song than Bowie ever had. And he gave maybe the greatest performance of his life when he turned Lead Belly's blues traditional "In the Pines" into a bottomless, raw-nerved yelp. He knocked the whole thing out in one take, with minimal stage banter, while going through withdrawal. The result: an image of a band at the height of its powers—as captured on the cover—taking on a pop institution but doing it their way. *MTV Unplugged in New York* is, in certain moments, my favorite Nirvana album. And it's the one that best shows what Cobain could have done if he hadn't let his demons claim him. Even when he wasn't hiding behind his band's overdriven scrape-roar, he was a presence that couldn't be shaken.

Like this?
Check out these three too

The Meat Puppets
Meat Puppets II

Pearl Jam
Yield

The Vaselines
Dying for It

OUTKAST STANKONIA

by Luke Winkie

There are plenty of frightening alternate realities to ponder, but more than any zombie apocalypse or ecological collapse, a universe where *Stankonia* was never made might actually suck the most. Where David Sheats never threaded that perfect, bouncing piano on "Ms. Jackson," and André 3000 didn't have the audacity to turn his breakup with Erykah Badu into his quintessential moment as a songwriter. Where Killer Mike missed his early, profane star-making moment on "Snappin' & Trappin'," and Big Boi couldn't quite fuse together the sublime, stutter-step "hold up, slow up, stop, control" on "B.O.B." There are better albums than *Stankonia* in this book, but none I cherish more.

There's not enough rap groups. There's never been enough rap groups. Collectives and partnerships always fizzle out, leaving behind one or two dominant voices and dozens of terrible solo albums stocked with confectionary guest verses. OutKast would suffer the same fate. *Stankonia* was released before *Speakerboxxx/The Love Below* and *Idlewild*—which both foreshadowed the band's breakup—and in 2006 they were gone. Sure, André and Big Boi returned in 2014 to play Coachella and gather some checks, but OutKast, *this OutKast*, are long dead. The teamwork; the kinship; the funky, odd-couple chemistry; the uniting under their own flag (like the reimagined American flag on the cover); the willingness to mix drum and bass twitches, chunky Hendrix guitar wails, and everything in between with total bravery and confidence—we'll never hear that again.

Should we be surprised? As much as we might wish that these two ATLiens could bury their differences and return to that same hyper-saturated well, *Stankonia*'s primary appeal might be just how rare it sounds. For exactly one moment in 2000, two of the world's greatest rappers combined their powers for a massive, unruly, 73-minute fit. Nothing about that is casual or replaceable. Afterward they had nothing more to give. If they've found peace, maybe we should too.

Like this?
Check out these three too

**Busta Rhymes
When Disaster Strikes**

**Future
DS2**

**Goodie Mob
Soul Food**

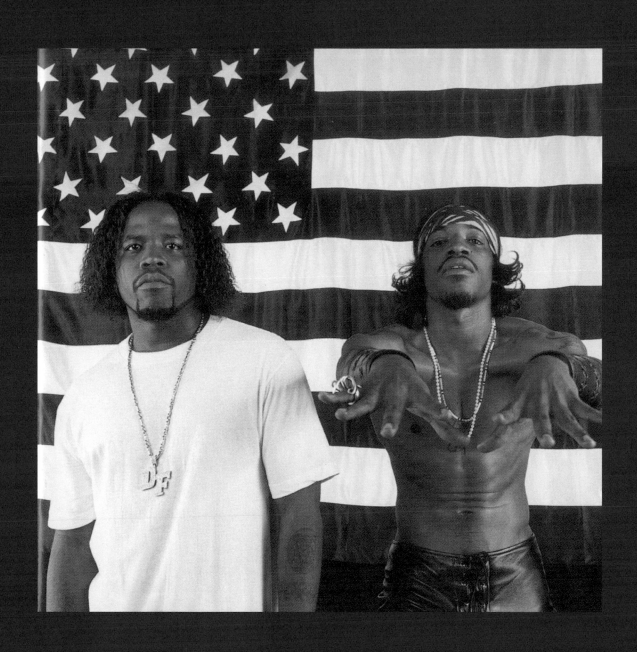

PAVEMENT
SLANTED AND ENCHANTED

by Luke Winkie

Has there ever been an indie-rock band that didn't want to be Pavement? Since *Slanted and Enchanted* dropped in '92, their stoned, slack-jawed, sarcastic goofiness has been the formula for every neurotic, pizzacore collective since. The origin story, in which a directionless Stephen Malkmus returns home to California and pieces together a couple of slapdash sessions with childhood friend Scott Kannberg and a degenerate session drummer with absolutely no expectations, has become the defining saga for the entire genre. Even the typography on the slapdash cover still resonates! Take a look at the track listing and feel the weird energy of all those little microscopic notebook koans—"Perfume-V," "Summer Babe (Winter Version)," "Zurich is Stained." The scene has been trying to capture that exact same disaffection ever since, and it's impossible, because nobody lacked self-consciousness quite like Pavement.

In the years since, Pavement went on to record a handful of great albums like *Wowee Zowee* and *Crooked Rain, Crooked Rain*, and write songs like "Cut Your Hair" that were imbued with a hilariously bitter cynicism toward the music industry at large. That's all great, but it will never be *Slanted and Enchanted*. Because *Slanted and Enchanted* didn't have the perspective or candor to be worried about external forces. Goofy, fuzzy, messy, full of delirious spoken-word meandering, drunken shredding, Malkmus's half-singing, and Kannberg's not-singing, remarkably plaintive ballads like "Here," and remarkable nothings like "Conduit for Sale!" It is the greatest indie-rock album ever made, and it was so confounding on release that most critics tried to compare them to Nirvana, which sounds super overbearing and inaccurate in retrospect. Pavement have always sounded like Pavement, and so does everyone else.

Like this?
Check out these three too

Built to Spill
Perfect From Now On

Guided by Voices
Alien Lanes

Yo La Tengo
Painful

PIXIES
SURFER ROSA

by Chris Lay

On their debut album, 1988's *Surfer Rosa*, the Pixies leapt straight out of the gate with their uniquely creepy confidence fully intact. Opening track "Bone Machine" ends its first verse with Frank Black stepping back from the mic and almost screaming, "You're so pretty when you're unfaithful to me," and we're off and running. They had been together as a band for a couple of years, and their tape of demos had resulted in the overstuffed *Come on Pilgrim* EP, but *Surfer Rosa* was their first barbaric yawp of a full length.

It's hard to not see *Surfer Rosa* as confrontational about the sorts of antisocial things you hear about but don't discuss (the half-naked woman on the cover surrounded by Catholic symbolism only serves to reinforce this impression). "Broken Face" is a frankly casual song that sketches a story of incest, "Gigantic" (sung by bassist Kim Deal) is a playfully sweet little ditty about the joys of experimenting with interracial sex seemingly for its own sake, and "Cactus" finds the narrator desperately longing for a woman to send him a bloody dress. There's even a bit of studio banter between band members Frank Black and Kim Deal, joking about a teacher abusing the members of his high school lacrosse team. These would be some tough pills to swallow if the songs weren't wonderfully jagged surf sketches cranked up to eleven. The album also has a song that opens with "This is a song about a superhero named Tony/It's called Tony's Theme," and then goes on to treat the act of riding a bike as if it were some literal superhuman ability, so things balance out in the end.

It's hard to imagine a world where this album doesn't exist. You take this thing out of circulation and you run the risk of no Radiohead, no Weezer, no Smashing Pumpkins, and on. Kurt Cobain himself says, "I was basically trying to rip off the Pixies," with regard to writing "Smells Like Teen Spirit," and it's probably not a coincidence that he enlisted *Surfer Rosa* producer Steve Albini to be behind the boards for *In Utero*. Beyond its legacy as an influence, though, *Surfer Rosa* just grabs at a somehow relatable twisted take on childhood and loss of innocence, but moves along happily fast enough to never get dragged down by how heavy a concept that is.

Like this? Check out these three too

The Breeders
Pod

Dinosaur Jr.
You're Living All Over Me

Nirvana
Nevermind

Pixies

Demtro las piñones y las holas 'riqueña. Oh my golly! Oh my golly! Caminamos bagala luna caribe. Oh my golly! Oh my golly!
Besando, chichando con Surfer Rosa. Oh my golly! Oh my golly! Entonces se fue en fus madera. Oh my golly! Oh my golly!
Rosa, oh oh ohh Rosa! Rosa, oh oh ohh Rosa! Yo soy playero pero no hay playa. Oh my golly! Oh my golly!
Bien perdida la Surfer Rosa. Oh my golly! Oh my golly! La vida total es un porkeria. Oh my golly! Oh my golly!
Me hecho menos más que vida. Oh my golly! Oh my golly! Rosa, oh oh ohh Rosa! Huh! Huh! Rosa, oh oh ohh Rosa! Huh! Huh!

PORTISHEAD
THIRD

by Ben Munson

Befuddlement with 45-rpm LPs can throw off a first encounter with Portishead's third album. The aptly titled and simply covered *Third* touched down 11 years after the Bristol band's previous album and, given that lengthy break, was likely to appear as an inevitable departure from the trip-hop genre they helped pioneer with their precisely Zeitgeist-tuned debut, *Dummy*. To distance themselves from the sinister break beats and record scratches of their work in the previous decade, maybe Portishead went full doom sludge?

Those are the thoughts that bounce through the brain until halfway through album-opener "Silence," when singer Beth Gibbons's unmistakable voice comes in and you instantly know you have the record playing on the wrong speed. So you move the needle back and hear "Silence" in the appropriate manner, as a nerve-wracking narrative of a crumbling relationship described by Gibbons, whose voice is the very muse of depression, sent to cave in chest cavities with exquisite pain.

Portishead's music has always blended melancholy with intrigue—if the band's self-titled 1997 album had come out in 2015 there likely would have been a White House petition demanding "All Mine" be the soundtrack to Daniel Craig's brooding James Bond. That ambience persists on *Third*, particularly within the sensual space conjured by the languidly paced strums and guitar melodies that bend around invasive transmissions on "Hunter," and on "Nylon Smile," where Gibbons pleads, "I don't know what I've done to deserve you," like glass shards hitting a tile floor.

The opening moments of *Third* provide a comforting callback to Portishead's previous music, but that familiarity digs deeper pitfalls further down the path for listeners convinced the band hadn't deviated too far from the genre it helped create. Geoff Barrow and Adrian Utley manage without much more than a gently plucked banjo on "The Rip" and let that dreary security carry through to the steady drone of "We Carry On," before opening the curtains on the sunny ukulele of "Deep Water." But it all seems like a beguiling setup once "Machine Gun" starts tenderizing soft tissue with an industrial-strength solution of drum machines and future-shock power electronics.

The further into *Third* you move, the clearer it becomes that Portishead not only successfully restarted after an eternal hiatus but also managed to modify their existence and amplify their relevance without entirely jettisoning everything that made them so vital in the first place.

Like this?
Check out these three too

Björk
Homogenic

Tricky
Maxinquaye

UNKLE
Never, Never, Land

ELDERTHORN

Ingredients

1 fl oz (30ml) brandy

½ fl oz (15ml) St-Germain

½ fl oz (15ml) Cynar

ice

Method

Stir all the ingredients together
in a mixing glass. Strain into a
chilled cocktail glass and serve.

PRINCE
SIGN O' THE TIMES

by Tom Breihan

By 1987, Prince had proven just about everything a recording artist could possibly hope to prove. He'd become a dominant pop force, a maker of blockbusters that would pack floors at weddings for generations to come.

He'd been a transgressive icon, freaking out parents and making isolated androgynous kids feel less alone. He'd been a boundary-pushing pop craftsman, to the point where half the songs on the radio sounded like him—whether they were actually his songs, songs he'd gifted to other artists, or merely songs ripping him off. He'd become one of the greatest, most exciting live acts in pop history. He'd fused genres and audiences in combinations that nobody else had attempted. He had masses, tastemakers, and critics eating out of his hand. He had no worlds left to conquer. Almost.

If Prince were still hoping for one final accomplishment, it was this: he wanted to put out one album that would show absolutely everything he could do. That's what he did with *Sign O' the Times*, an album that he'd originally planned to release as a triple LP. (The philistines at his label convinced him to winnow it down to a double.) Funny thing about *Sign O' the Times*: it's just a hair shy of 80 minutes. It *could* fit on a single CD. But if you bought it on the new compact-disc format, it still came spread across two pieces of plastic. Prince didn't care if you were an early

adapter to this new tech. He wanted you to have the same experience that the vinyl buyers were having.

It's all there on *Sign O' the Times*, every last musical strain that Prince could possibly chase. "Housequake" is a James Brown-style party-funk rave-up. "U Got the Look" is a classic dance-pop workout. "Adore" is a squelchy, heavy-breathing slow jam. "Starfish and Coffee" is a sparkling singer-songwriter meditation. "The Ballad of Dorothy Parker" is immaculate, understated new wave. And "The Cross" is, quite simply, one of the greatest rock power ballads of the '80s, a decade that wasn't exactly light on great rock power ballads. He tries all these different styles, and he does them all about as well as they can possibly be done.

It should be as much of a mess as the cover, but Prince had an auteur's sense of control. So every element of the mix, even the crowds cheering on the 10-minute live vamp, "It's Gonna Be a Beautiful Night," feels like it's exactly in its right place. This was his first release since splitting with the Revolution, the band he'd made *Purple Rain* with, and he made much of it the way he made his early records: by playing every single instrument himself. The idea that a single human being could've produced an album this varied, expansive, and flat-out *great* should honestly make the rest of us feel terrible. Prince was a real human being. He really made this. So what are the rest of us doing with our lives?

Like this?
Check out these three too

The Gap Band
Gap Band IV

Michael Jackson
Dangerous

The Time
Ice Cream Castle

QUEENS OF THE STONE AGE

SONGS FOR THE DEAF

PARENTAL
ADVISORY
EXPLICIT CONTENT

QUEENS OF THE STONE AGE
SONGS FOR THE DEAF

by Andy O'Connor

A Big Rock Record, one unlike the Big Rock Records that came before it, and with this dude Dave Grohl just slaying it on the drums—no, not that one. This one came just under 11 years later, when the perceived enemy was no longer hair metal, but nu-metal and the spoiled seed of grunge's decaying remnants. (Grohl still profits off that with Foo Fighters, but, hey, your day job ain't that great either.) Josh Homme distilled the "desert sound" he pioneered in Kyuss into one of the last, maybe the last, Big Rock Records that kicked enough ass for the heshers and didn't skimp on the hooks or the ambition.

Songs for the Deaf is a record of CD-era length, clocking in around an hour, but one that doesn't overstay its welcome (most of our favorite bands can't even make 78-minute records great), with the diversity of an LP-era classic. Right out the gate, "Millionaire," where bassist and former partner in crime (this would be his second and last record with them) Nick Oliveri pumps out righteous stoner thrash too mean for Kyuss; "Six Shooter" is a concentrated repackaging, with Oliveri's screams even more maniacal.

Homme's always been the ringleader—he'd be the one throwing the pitchfork on the cover—still, *Deaf* is the best contrast of his smoothness with Oliveri's "fuck you up and get high" demeanor. Queens' other records are missing that, and, for all their strengths, it shows. "Go with the Flow" tacks the desert sound on to a Stooges-esque rhythmic pummel, complete with runaway piano straight out of *Raw Power*, and if your parents weren't cool enough to tell you about Iggy Pop's practically sprayed-on silver pants, it's close enough. The back to back of "A Song for the Dead" and "The Sky is Fallin'" gives shine to the druggier edge of the desert sound, with slower tempos that don't drag. And for all the garage-rock worship that was going on at the time, the Hives and the White Stripes couldn't pull off hit single "No One Knows" and the bittersweet "Another Love Song" if they tried.

Deaf wasn't just the last great Big Rock Record, but it also served as a funeral for the radio it ultimately wooed. Woven throughout are skits parodying various Southern California radio voids, from KLON—"clone radio"—to WOMB, the trippiest, perhaps stickiest new-age station around; they're supposed to make *Deaf* a concept album, but they're best viewed as brief respites in between some killer jams. In 2002, it was some of the best rock satire since Zappa's passing; now, we wish radio was even that interesting. Can you imagine your local huckster begging "Where's the saga? I need a saga!" in between movie-ticket giveaways and playing "Back in Black" for the umpteenth time? Didn't think so.

Like this? Check out these three too

Eagles of Death Metal
Peace, Love, Death Metal

Jane's Addiction
Nothing's Shocking

Wolfmother
Wolfmother

RADIOHEAD
AMNESIAC

by Levi J Sheppard and Joshua Lingenfelter

By the end of the millennium, Radiohead had achieved worldwide renown after releasing *Pablo Honey*, *The Bends*, and the huge cultural moment and critical success that was *OK Computer*. Free to explore the recesses of their minds during the recording sessions that yielded both *Kid A* and *Amnesiac*, Radiohead discovered a plethora of new material. What they found, as they ramped up the experimental elements and scoured the treasure chest of what music could be, were sounds both unsettling—many tracks hinting at the electronic dissonance that artists like Oneohtrix Point Never would later explore—and comforting.

Kid A ends with Thom Yorke singing, "I will see you in the next life"; *Amnesiac* begins with "After years of waiting, nothing came." The weeping minotaur on the cover art, produced by Yorke and Stanley Donwood, speaks to this sense of being lost with no hope of company. Although critics might claim *Amnesiac* is comprised of leftovers from the *Kid A* sessions, the depth and range of the material reveal otherwise. There are, however, easy parallels to draw between the two albums. "Pyramid Song" is a hauntingly beautiful track, one that speaks of Buddhist and scientific ideas of cyclical time, and that recalls "How to Disappear Completely" from

the prior album. "Hunting Bears," a short instrumental, which at first seems like simple, wandering guitar effects, ultimately makes for an interesting counterpoint to the short drone instrumental of *Kid A*'s "Treefingers." The song "Morning Bell" is found on both albums, and is reinterpreted with dramatic and looming variation on *Amnesiac*, further suggesting that these albums are meant to be considered as two sides of the same coin.

Amnesiac is not Radiohead's "best" album—it's certainly not their most popular or their most noteworthy release. Potentially the least accessible album in the towering Radiohead catalog, *Amnesiac* is Radiohead at peak impunity, enjoying the freedoms earned after the success of *OK Computer*. At first pass, a casual listener might be driven away, if fixated on the album's repetitive and dissonant elements—it is made up of 11 songs of different instruments, styles, and tempos—but it is important to note that these songs represent elements of Radiohead's entire career, from the rock anthems of their debut albums to Atoms for Peace and other multiple solo side projects. *Amnesiac*'s strength is in evoking deep emotion from the abstract vocals and experimental songwriting. The feelings elicited here are some of the strongest and strangest of the band's immense catalog.

Like this? Check out these three too

Burial
Untrue
(see pages 54–5)

The Flaming Lips
Yoshimi Battles the Pink Robots

Four Tet
Pink

RADIOHEAD
AMNESIAC

FELA RANSOME-KUTI AND THE AFRICA '70 WITH GINGER BAKER LIVE!

by Jes Skolnik

After dissolving the fiery partnership he had with bassist Jack Bruce that made Cream's rhythm section so tremendous (and so volatile), flitting in and out of former bandmate Eric Clapton's blues-rock supergroup Blind Faith, and trying his hand at jazz fusion with Ginger Baker's Air Force, what was the notoriously ornery and explosive "world's first superstar rock drummer" to do? Why, cut himself off from all of his former friends and move to Africa in search of new rhythmic inspiration, of course.

During his time in Africa, Baker struck up a friendship and creative partnership with popular Nigerian composer, vocalist, and bandleader Fela Kuti, who had recently found new inspiration for his Afrobeat sound on a long trip to Los Angeles, where he'd been introduced to the Black Panther Party and American black nationalism in general. Upon returning to Nigeria, Kuti shifted his music's focus and style, from poppy highlife love songs to funky, jazzy improvisations mostly concerned with politics and society ("Black Man's Cry" in particular is a post-colonial rallying cry to the entire African diaspora). This 1971 live album sees Kuti fully developing and refining the stylistic formula he used through the '70s and '80s: extended jams (most over 10 minutes) that fuse traditional Ghanaian and Nigerian folk music, jazz, and James Brown–style funk soul into a heady mix with long instrumental breaks and call-and-response vocals. "Egbe Mi O (Carry Me I Want to Die)" is a fine study in the value of the folk song broken apart and turned into ruthless funk vamp.

Baker brings his characteristic dynamic, complex, hard-hitting style to bear on this recording, but he's not the center of the composition by any means. This is a Fela Kuti record, an Africa '70 record, before it is a Ginger Baker record (the album's cover, and the bonus track, which is a drum battle between Baker and fellow star drummer Tony Allen, notwithstanding). Baker is just part of the band here rather than a standout iconoclast, a role he seems to relish (in the documentary *Beware of Mr. Baker*, he hints that it may have been a relief to take a backseat to Kuti, another charismatic performer, after Baker's contentious time in the British rock spotlight). Kuti was a populist, often singing in pidgin English so that his songs would communicate across African national and regional language barriers, and this is a populist record, meant for dancing *and* consciousness-raising.

Like this?
Check out these three too

Antibalas
Antibalas

Hugh Masekela
Masekela

King Sunny Ade
Vintage

173

THE REPLACEMENTS
LET IT BE

by Sarah Sahim

They say imitation is the best form of flattery, and for the Replacements this is best manifested in their odes to the musicians who shaped them. In this instance, their third record was named after the famous Beatles single, "Let It Be." Upon listening to any of the Replacements' records, the Beatles' soft, accessible melodies might not immediately come across as one of lead singer's Paul Westerberg's influences, but they had everyone from Hank Williams to Big Star to thank for their sound.

Let It Be was a step up in terms of artistic maturity. Their debut record, *Sorry Ma, Forgot to Take Out the Trash*, was this heavy and hardcore adrenaline rush of a record with danceable numbers like "Otto," and their follow-up, *Hootenanny*, though more expansive, was still slapdash. The bouncy and piano-laden singalong "Androgynous" sees the band tackling gender-based stereotypes and has become something of a genderqueer anthem in more recent years, cemented by Miley Cyrus, Joan Jett, and Laura Jane Grace covering it. So many people find solace in the Replacements because they represented the weirdos and outcasts of society, which the cover illustrates: these are the kind of guys who don't sit on your couch, but will sit on your porch roof because they can.

This is an uncomfortable record, and that's one of its standout attributes. Westerberg's songs most notably revolve around his belief that he is a broken man—too broken to fix—and the Replacements' lyrics were his therapy. On "Gary's Got a Boner," he sings (presumably to himself), "C'mon little Gary, get your head on right/C'mon little Gary, get your head on straight," but with that signature cheeky wit, it's contextualized with the song's subject having an uncontrollable erection.

An iconic line from the Beatles song "Let It Be" is "When I find myself in times of trouble Mother Mary comes to me/Speaking words of wisdom." The song rests on this notion that beneath the chaos of life lies a spiritual serenity. The Replacements operated on the opposite of this, though. Westerberg painfully sang through his gruffness on "Unsatisfied" that "Everything you dream of/Is right in front of you/And everything is a lie/And liberty is a lie." And yet, nihilism notwithstanding, the Replacements still managed to keep their chins somewhat up. Westerberg is a funny guy, and could see right through people's bullshit. "Seen your video, the phony rock 'n' roll/We don't want to know." The Replacements were chaos, anarchy, and just tried to make do with what they had.

Like this?
Check out these three too

**Hüsker Dü
Zen Arcade**

**Minutemen
Double Nickels
on the Dime**

**Mission of Burma
Vs.**

THE ROLLING STONES
STICKY FINGERS

by Drew Millard

To be a true fan of the Rolling Stones is to understand that a good chunk of the band's discography is total bullshit. Lots of their old stuff is bad, pretty much all of the new stuff is bad, but there was a distinct period, from *Beggars Banquet* up until *Goats Head Soup*, where Mick, Keef, and the boys were the greatest goddamn band in all of rock 'n' roll. The group had become masters of the art of capturing that perfect feeling of freedom one gets from skating on the razor's edge, throwing caution to the wind, and laughing in the face of whatever horrific damage you might be about to inflict upon yourself. It goes without saying that recording records with a brazen sense of fuck-it-all tends to not lend itself to recording flawless albums; one might argue that this is one of the reasons why this era of Stones material has such a distinct sense of ramshackle charm that is impossible to re-create.

Still, the Stones were only the titans of their era in retrospect. Before the recording of *Sticky Fingers*, the band had inadvertently presided over the death of Ken Kesey's hippie dream, performing at the disastrous December 1969 Altamont Free Concert, in which some Hells Angels working security killed Meredith Hunter and the idealism of

the '60s along with him. They owed their label Decca one last single—which they delivered in the form of "Cocksucker Blues," the rudest, crudest, and most half-assed track they could muster, which was refused by Decca on general principle. Then, rather than saying, "Hey, sorry we killed the '60s," the Stones put out *Sticky Fingers*, a record with a life-size close-up of some guy's crotch—complete with zipper and belt buckle that damaged records around it in the stacks—on the cover.

As luck would have it, beneath the zipper lay considerable greatness. There was "Brown Sugar," perhaps *the* quintessential Rolling Stones stomper. "Wild Horses," "Sister Morphine," and "Moonlight Mile" were stabs at elegiac beauty the band had only hinted at on previous records. And with lead guitarist Mick Taylor—fresh from a stint with John Mayall's Bluesbreakers—having fully replaced Brian Jones on guitar, the Stones were able to inject their tunes with a breezy, bluesy swing that set them apart from every other group of drunk British dudes throwing up on each other. *Sticky Fingers* may not be the definitive Stones record, but it's probably their best. And for a group of guys who seemed to love trying to not try, that's pretty impressive.

Like this?
Check out these three too

The Brian Jonestown Massacre
Thank God for Mental Illness

Derek and the Dominos
Layla and Other Assorted Love Songs

The Jimi Hendrix Experience
Electric Ladyland

RUSH
MOVING PICTURES

by Andy O'Connor

If you subscribe to conventional music-crit history, you may think that rock got too bloated (no other synonym will do), and punk saved us all from suites of excess. Three chords and anyone could start a band in New York '77, hurray! No more of this progressive-rock shit! In reality, Rush didn't give a fuck about punk, and *Moving Pictures* showed that they were definitely leaner and maybe meaner than the snotty kids trying to take them down.

Pop smarts always laid hidden in them; "Fly by Night" and "Working Man" are solid hard-rock jams, even if they're just less sophisticated Zeppelin. "Closer to the Heart" proved they could write radio bangers congruent with their own identity, and *Permanent Waves* showed they could stretch that ability out to an album's length. *Pictures* is one of those rare records where they're three steps ahead of everyone else, refining their instrumental mastery, sharpening their editing, and becoming even more of a sponge to various influence while maintaining their own stamp on prog. Alex Lifeson still brings big energy to knotty arrangements, Geddy Lee still attacks with his unmistakable wail, and Neil Peart still bashes forth with intricacy amateurs are still trying to master years later—it's just all more compact, and as a result a brainy band gets even smarter (just look at the triple meaning of the album title and cover art: physically moving pictures, pictures that are emotionally moving, and moving pictures, as in a motion movie).

"YYZ" serves as both a primer for their instrumental glory and an affirmation that a vocal-less jam could be a staple on rock radio. It's a prog suite with the sensibility of a pop song—bombastic (not unusual for prog) and highly hummable (huh?). *Pictures* came out when new wave was beginning to take off, and it features more synthesizer flourishes from Lee, but the latter was not caused by the former. All of the songs rule, but "Limelight" is one of those once-in-a-lifetime songs a band hopes to whip forth. It's a meditation on anxiety and privacy—or specifically Peart's—disguised as a carefree rock jam. Sadness lightly coats but never suffocates; Lifeson's solo constantly rises in a way that suggests he's actually making his guitar cry on Peart's behalf. It's redeemed in joy by Peart's ending salvo, concentrated blasts that affirm that he can embrace the difficulties of fame.

The darkness underlying "Limelight" takes over the second half of the record, culminating in "Vital Signs," where Lifeson's reggae-influenced guitars serve as a foil for Lee's busy bass and swirling synths. Rush has always been particularly influential on metal over the years, and "Witch Hunt," with its brooding tempos and ominous synths, is an underrated example of such. If you've thought of Rush as shrill and excessive, *Pictures* will convince you to change your mind. Yeah, the nerds can and will rock way harder than you ever will.

Like this? Check out these three too

Blue Öyster Cult
Agents of Fortune

Boston
Boston

ZZ Top
Eliminator

S-Z

GIL SCOTT-HERON
SMALL TALK AT 125TH AND LENOX

by Michael Penn II

When the needle dropped, Heron found a way to teleport the listener to 125th and Lenox instantaneously; for all the grit, despair, prevalence, and hope. Congo lines thrive in their minimalism for most of the 42-minute runtime, giving Heron's voice the space to meditate when he must and be enraged when no one else will. There isn't a smidgen of hesitation to drive every syllable through the heart of Lady Liberty and her constituents.

This album is a murderer; it cares not of how you beg forgiveness. Heron will condemn you of your crimes and sentence you to damnation. You may even smile as he lowers the guillotine.

The Harlem he spoke of then may look much different now: the project building may be swapped for condominiums with a Whole Foods underneath, and the black folks are slowly disappearing. Take this album as the true snapshot it is: the street corner as a metaphor for the nation. Harlem is the center of the universe, and a college degree is neither prerequisite nor qualifier for the revolution. Hell, you can't hashtag the revolution in 1970. If you aren't in it to dismantle the evils he sees every day—to remove needles from veins and put food in every mouth without it—Heron insists that you get the fuck out of the way. White or otherwise.

Small Talk at 125th and Lenox will depress you because it will not sound dated in the slightest. Our dead bodies are still black. Dope is in the medicine cabinet and the Styrofoam. We still spend more on war than on the poor. This record will make you pray for the day that records like it, decades after their creation, won't narrate such turmoil so effectively.

Heron's homophobic and patriarchal moments are disheartening reflections of the era. (Tragically, many of these tropes hold true in the hip-hop we know several decades later.) How fitting for Heron to stand as a precursor to the hip-hop movement's inception: an unflinching voice in the chaos, staring out from the album's stark cover, leaving no one out of the crossfire, even when it's dead wrong. If you want to hear where everyone from Kanye to "King Kunta" can credit their swagger, *125th and Lenox* is a requirement.

Like this?
Check out these three too

Miles Davis
On the Corner

The Last Poets
The Last Poets

Buddy Miles
Them Changes

A New Black Poet
GIL SCOTT-HERON
Small Talk at 125th and Lenox

Gil Scott-Heron takes you Inside Black. Inside, where the anger burns against *The Ones Who* "broke my family tree." Inside, where the black man sorts his miseries "while white men walk on stars."

He penetrates to the core, where, blurred by the "plastic patterns" of a culture not his own, dulled by drugs, or held down by unremitting poverty, the Black's rage smolders, ready to flare into riot.

In *Small Talk at 125th and Lenox*, Gil Scott-Heron, twenty-year-old poet, speaks for his people with an eloquence that has won him recognition as a major new talent. His is the voice of the new black man, rebellious and proud, demanding to be heard, announcing his destiny: "I AM COMING!"

Flying Dutchman

STEREO FD 10131

SIGUR RÓS
TAKK...

by Jes Skolnik

Before *Takk...*, it was perhaps easier to write off Sigur Rós as being one-trick post-rock ponies or to pack them off into easy mythology—*of course* their sound is otherworldly and glacial, sad and strange. Just look at the eerily pretty cover art with the ghost-like figure of a young boy. They're from *Iceland*: have you seen the Northern Lights; have you heard *Björk*? It was easy, with their minimal design and lyrics sung in Icelandic or their own glossolalic tongue, to project our own ideas about who they were onto them.

Takk..., though, is sun-dappled and human-scale, a full and bright orchestral-rock record that channels the band's signature elements—Jónsi Birgisson's cello-bowed guitar and falsetto vocals, Kjartan Sveinsson's careful orchestral arrangements and choir-like keyboards, the whole band's complex and mathematical time signature changes threading the bones of their songwriting like snake vertebrae—into something eminently gentle and joyful. The essential grimness and stiff procession-type melodies of some of their previous work secede in favor of the twinkling, catchy phrases of "Glósóli" and the piano play of "Hoppípolla." It is still airier and more minimal than some of their later, even more accessible work, but *Takk...* is a real benchmark for Sigur Rós. It is the moment when all of our preconceived notions about who Sigur Rós were failed.

The first time I heard *Takk...* in full was shortly after its release, at a friend's house. We were sitting cross-legged on her floor, discussing our respective struggles with depression. We were talking about how when you're depressed the edges of every day feel dull and your tongue feels stuck, and how strange it felt, when you've been living with depression for so long, to feel the absence of those visceral pulls. She got up to flip the record, and the chimes of the intro to "Sé Lest" filled the room, followed by the swell of strings. We were silent for a minute, looking at each other, listening, both struck by the delicacy of the composition. The room was dark, but it felt lit from within with a sort of golden warmth. "It's weird to feel glad to be alive," I said. And, in that moment, it was true.

Like this?
Check out these three too

Explosions in the Sky
The Earth Is Not a Cold Dead Place

Mogwai
Happy Songs for Happy People

múm
Summer Make Good

THE WINK

Ingredients

½ fl oz (15ml) absinthe

1½ fl oz (45ml) gin

⅓ fl oz (10ml) triple sec

½ fl oz (15ml) simple syrup

2 dashes of Peychaud's bitters

ice

orange peel

Method

Rinse a lowball glass with the absinthe. Combine the gin, triple sec, simple syrup, and bitters in an ice-filled cocktail shaker. Shake vigorously and strain into the absinthe-rinsed glass. Twist the orange peel over the top of the drink to release the oils, discard, and serve.

PAUL SIMON GRACELAND

by Ben Munson

The controversy surrounding Paul Simon's *Graceland* never reached my home when I was young. To me, a small man—relative to Chevy Chase—had made music both exotic and familiar, a colorful album that made my mom blush and sway. It was an introduction to the idea of world music. That was it. But with information that resurfaced in Joe Berlinger's film documenting the making of *Graceland* on the album's 25th anniversary, it's believable that Simon's 1986 full-length played some part in ending apartheid in South Africa.

Simon had said to hell with a United Nations cultural boycott and in 1985 traveled to Johannesburg to record with some township jive and Sotho traditional musicians, all because he heard a song he liked on a mixtape. In South Africa he borrowed inspiration and sounds from the Boyoyo Boys and General M.D. Shirinda and the Gaza Sisters, for songs like "Gumboots" and "I Know What I Know," while finding the footing to push forward powerful rhythms on "The Boy in the Bubble" and "Graceland" with the help of genius contributors guitarist Ray Phiri and fretless bass player Bakithi Kumalo*.

Those four songs form a foundation for Simon to let off frantic forewarnings of bleak technological futures, estrangement, and vapid conversations while permitting us to dance. But you're forgiven if your familiarity with *Graceland* strengthens closer to the middle of the album because your mother, as was her right since she bought the record and owned the stereo, always skipped ahead to "Diamonds on the Soles of Her Shoes" and let it play through "You Can Call Me Al."

The gemstone-forsaking meet cute and the alias-imploring alienation tale, assisted by Ladysmith Black Mambazo's vocal melodies, and more crystalline guitars and rubbery rhythms from Phiri and Kumalo, end up bridging sides one and two of the *Graceland*'s vinyl release.

The back half of *Graceland* doesn't short on highlights including "Under African Skies"—the Linda Ronstadt duet describes a Zulu walking rhythm by producer Hilton Rosenthal—as well as Zydeco sendup "That Was Your Mother" and the Los Lobos-assisted "All Around the World or the Myth of Fingerprints."

But those songs don't similarly capture the imagination like Simon's work with South African musicians. He busted a serious boycott and offered a glimpse of the humanity surrounding critical problems half a world away, disguised as music that always made my mom ask me to dance with her.

*He got the cover from an Ethiopian depiction of Saint George. Paul got all over Africa for *Graceland*.

Like this?
Check out these three too

Ladysmith Black Mambazo
Inkazimulo

Orchestre Du Bawobab
Ndeleng Ndeleng

Vampire Weekend
Vampire Weekend

PAUL · SIMON
GRACELAND

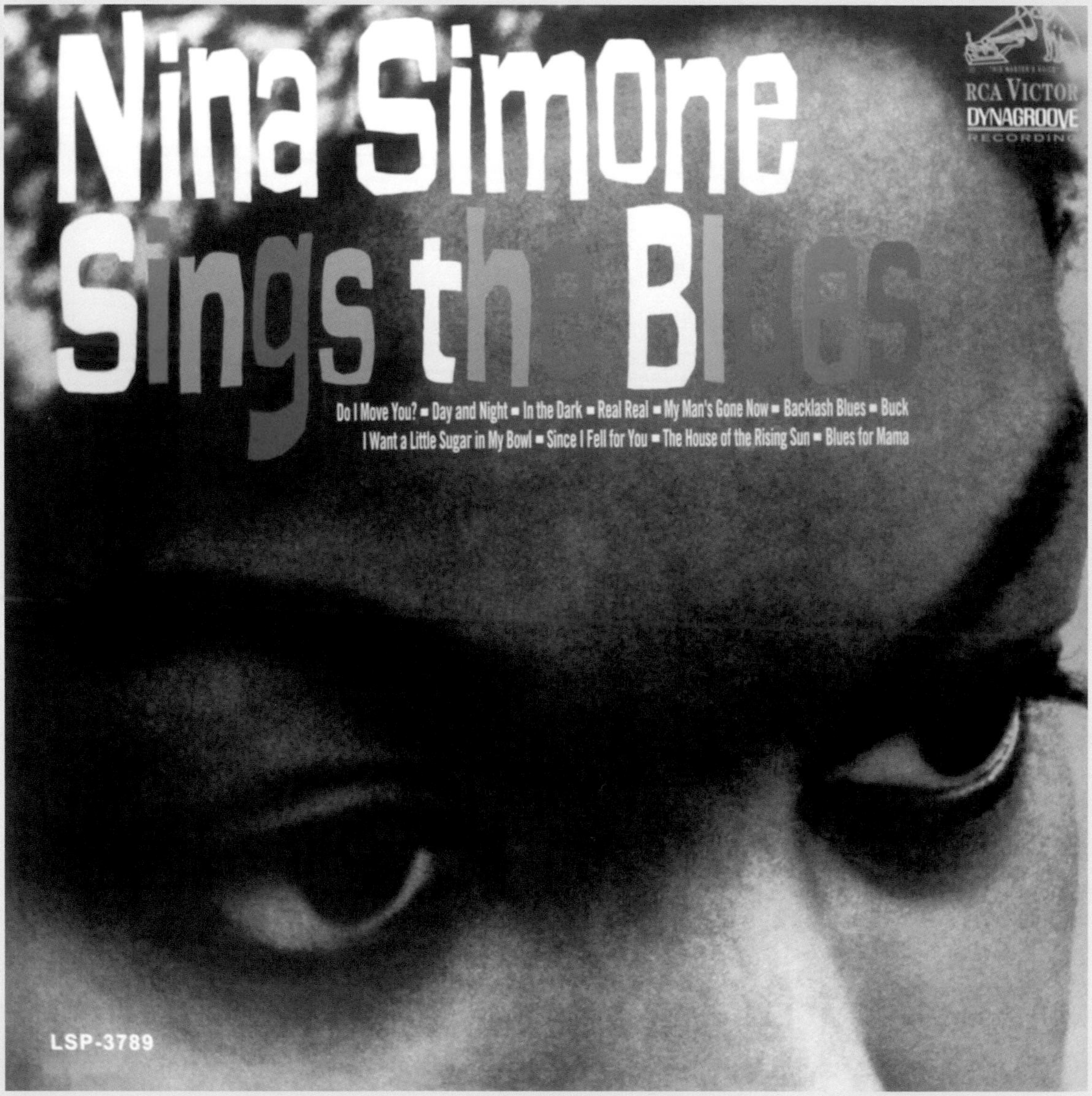
Nina Simone
Sings the Blues
RCA Victor
DYNAGROOVE
Do I Move You? ▪ Day and Night ▪ In the Dark ▪ Real Real ▪ My Man's Gone Now ▪ Backlash Blues ▪ Buck
I Want a Little Sugar in My Bowl ▪ Since I Fell for You ▪ The House of the Rising Sun ▪ Blues for Mama
LSP-3789

NINA SIMONE
NINA SIMONE SINGS THE BLUES

by Geoff Rickly

○

Those looking to dive into the deep waters of Nina Simone's catalog face a daunting challenge: a handful of her records could be considered *the* classic masterwork. *I Put a Spell on You* leans furthest in the direction of pop and delivers some of her most well-loved songs, with "Feeling Good," the title track, and "Ne Me Quitte Pas" all earning their place in the modern canon. *Pastel Blue* breaks challenging with the 10-minute marathon "Sinnerman" and her vital political interpretation of "Strange Fruit." Later, *Wild is the Wind* practically laid out the map for sad singer-songwriters like Cat Power. In the words of feminist icon Germaine Greer, "Every generation has to discover Nina Simone."

To discover Simone at her most essential, start with *Nina Simone Sings the Blues*. The cover image narrows in on Simone's intent gaze, revealing a singular focus that could be the byword for the album. By stripping away the sometimes schmaltzy string sections and unnecessarily baroque arrangements of her Philips recordings, Simone's golden voice emerges through the smoke in all its naked glory: full-throated and self-assured on "Do I Move You?," direct and disenfranchised on the politically charged "Backlash Blues"(penned by her friend and Harlem Renaissance leader Langston Hughes), and most notably authoritative, androgynous, and dripping with sexuality on the "I Want a Little Sugar in My Bowl."

Simone's small pickup band delivers a proficient blues performance, succeeding by hugging tight to the tempo and feel of Simone's expressive piano work, which is to say they were smart enough to do as little as possible. Similarly, the record's intimate tone best captures moments when you can sense the players gathered around Simone, waiting for her to lock into a groove, pick a key, and set the song on fire. In these moments, the drums jump in joyful surprise and the sax squeals in laughter at her most audacious provocations, such as how to keep a man happy in "Day and Night": "Even when he's wrong, tell him that he's right/ You can take the blame both day and night."

The inescapable truth of *Sings the Blues*, evident in every inimitable performance, is that modern music would be absolutely bereft without Simone.

Like this? Check out these three too

Ella Fitzgerald
Lullabies of Birdland

Aretha Franklin
Young, Gifted and Black

Billie Holiday
Lady Sings the Blues

ELLIOTT SMITH
EITHER/OR

by Susannah Young

Watching a person during a period of transition in their life is the closest we ever get to experiencing time in a nonlinear way; in each moment, we can see the ghost of who they used to be and the shape of everything they'll one day become. And because artists produce physical evidence documenting the contents of their minds, tectonic shifts in their lives are all the more interesting to observe, since their breadcrumb trail of creative output offers context through which to view what came before and what will come after.

This is the enduring appeal of albums like *Either/Or*, which was a transitional point for Elliott Smith in so many ways. It's the album where he first applied the Technicolor treatment to his one-man band, where multi-tracked vocals and instrumentals put meat on the bones of his songs—a choice he continued to make with increasing artistic and financial investment on subsequent albums *XO* and *Figure 8*. It's an album he recorded while he was still in Heatmiser, but had left the band by the time he released it. It's the album that netted him widespread notoriety and thousands more fans, thanks to Gus Van Sant cherry-picking the album's most relevant songs to fill out the *Good Will Hunting* soundtrack, resolving in a rattled-looking Smith performing "Miss Misery" at the 1997 Oscars, dressed in a gleaming white suit.

It's also the album where Smith poignantly documents his own betweenness through some of his most thoughtfully rendered characters: the self-shaming that follows uncomfortable self-reflection ("Alameda" and also the album's back-to-the-mirror cover); a transcript of a poisonous relationship characterized by mutually enabling self-destructive behavior ("Between the Bars"); the title track's ricocheting between past and future, put-on personas, dreams, and reality. The album feels the way it feels to live life: never having all the context you need to handle a situation with the utmost confidence, to feel like you're living the way you'd want to live or should be living, or to repair the quiet damage you've done to your own life and the lives of those around you.

Like this?
Check out these three too

Bright Eyes
I'm Wide Awake, It's Morning

Sparklehorse
It's a Wonderful Life

M. Ward
Transfiguration of Vincent

Elliott Smith

Patti Smith Horses

PATTI SMITH
HORSES

by Tom Breihan

"Jesus died for somebody's sins, but not mine. My sins are my own. They belong to me." *That* is a motherfuck of a way to start your first album. When people talk about Patti Smith's *Horses* today, they tend to do so in the context of that legendarily messy first wave of New York punk—or, worse, about the whole women-in-rock talking point, tired 20 years ago and unforgivably reductionist today. The women-in-rock thing doesn't merit discussion—the iconic Mapplethorpe image of Smith on the cover was a radical departure from the image of most female singers at the time but, as Smith noted, "That's just the way I dressed." The punk thing? Smith played the same clubs as the Ramones and their buddies, and she knew all those guys. But while she might've been *from* that, she wasn't *of* it. That much is clear from the first line. She had bigger things on her mind.

Horses isn't anything so small as a look at a genre in its zygote stage. Instead, it's a declaration of self, a radical retelling of rock myths that put Rimbaud and Fats Domino on equal footing. Smith wasn't a punk—not really. Instead, she belonged to a rare strain of rock-mystic furies—a subspecies that includes Robert Plant and Iggy Pop, and maybe a couple of other people. Smith was a revered writer before she even picked up a mic, so maybe we should just group her with Leonard Cohen and nobody else.

There's an elemental thud to the music on *Horses*. Lenny Kaye, Smith's guitarist, was more writer than musician, but he was the world's leading scholar in hammerhead '60s garage rock, and he knew how to put his minimal skills to work. Producer John Cale was fresh off his time in the Velvet Underground, and he injected the album with some of his old band's scraping, paranoiac intensity. But everything fed off Smith—not just off her words but also off the unhinged, free-floating way she used that world-swallowing voice.

Consider "Land," the album's nine-minute centerpiece. As it opens, all we hear is Smith's voice, breathlessly recounting a story of a high school hallway fight. And as it builds, the focus shifts. Johnny, her narrator, catches visions of horses and Rimbaud and "Land of 1,000 Dances" and knives and cocaine and a place called space. And as we disappear into his head, the literal disappears, and that frantic, riveting free association is all that remains. No other performer in rock history, before or since, could've pulled off a performance like this, just as nobody else could've started off her debut like *that*.

Like this?
Check out these three too

Bob Dylan
Slow Train Coming

Marianne Faithfull
Marianne Faithfull

Richard Hell and the Voidoids
Blank Generation

THE SMITHS
THE QUEEN IS DEAD

by Eric Sundermann

The Queen Is Dead, the Smiths' third record, which was released in 1986, is the English band's best in a discography full of albums better than most other musicians can ever dream of recording. It features our pal Morrissey, somehow both the saddest and most pretentious man who's ever walked the planet (it's no surprise that it was Morrissey who designed the cover, featuring a still of Alain Delon in French film, *L'Insoumis*), in his finest form. Despite ruminating on the Big Ideas™ like media obsession ("The Queen Is Dead"), death ("Cemetry Gates"), or the end of a relationship ("I Know It's Over"), the unbearable holier-than-thou tone that would infect Morrissey's later career is balanced well with his quips and smartass remarks.

Listening with fresh ears, you forget that the singer is such an enormous dickhead whose political beliefs have come to define him, at times, more than the music he made to get famous—and, believe it or not, on *The Queen Is Dead*, he actually does come across as quite the charming man.

Let's look at the lyrics of "There Is a Light That Never Goes Out," probably the most popular Smiths song that's ever been recorded, and a track that will forever soundtrack the romance of people who dress well and believe they're hip. "If a double decker bus crashes into us/To die by your side is such a heavenly way to die." There's a sort of beauty in the glibness with which Morrissey sings, embracing the inevitable doom of human existence while pairing it with the blind joy of human connection. There's certain nihilism in *The Queen Is Dead*, a bizarre, hedonistic approach to the way we think about ourselves—the end is near, life is worthless, why even bother to go outside because nothing really does matter and we're all doomed forever. But, then again, maybe that's just what it's like to be English.

Like this?
Check out these three too

**Echo and the Bunnymen
Ocean Rain**

**New Order
Power, Corruption & Lies**

**U2
The Joshua Tree**

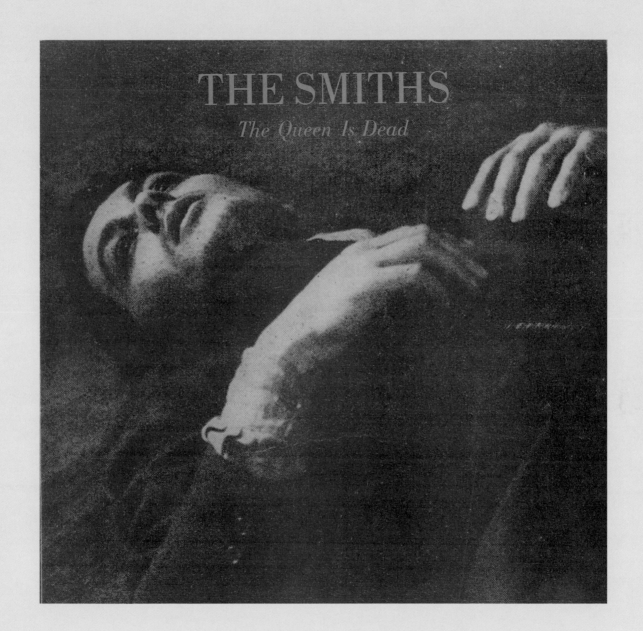

Spiritualized®

Ladies and gentlemen we are floating in space B P

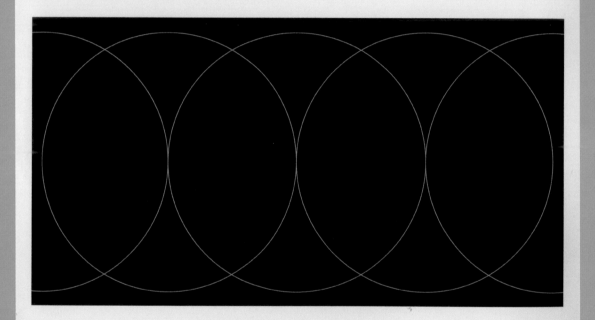

2 tablets 70 min

SPIRITUALIZED
LADIES AND GENTLEMEN WE ARE FLOATING IN SPACE

by Geoff Rickly

I have a picture that I save in case life gets too grim to go on. It's a black-and-white picture taken at the *Ladies and Gentlemen We Are Floating in Space* exhibit at the Creators Project. The picture is of a blind child, standing in a shaft of light, face to the sky, listening intently to J Spaceman's otherworldly guitars spin all around him, in absolute rapture.

The song floats in on the hazy guitars that early Spiritualized (and Spacemen 3 before them) built their name on, but quickly builds with dovetailed strings and a choir of singers. Resisting resolution, the song stretches out infinitely, like a modern "Pachelbel's Canon." It speaks to the endless dimensions of heartbreak, but also the endless euphoria that comes from making music to cure heartbreak.

The record is by turns gloriously triumphant ("Come Together") and shockingly spare ("Broken Heart"). But whether J Spaceman is detailing "Driving fast down a one-way street/ Lord of loving you dance so sweet/Going fast to hit the sky," ("Electricity"), or explaining that "Little Johnny's sad and fucked/First he jumped and then he looked/The tracks of time/Those tracks of mine," ("Come Together"), his guitar is always expressive, booming the thunder of wide-open highways, blurring past, or melting like the sick light of the hospital emergency room.

If the intricately layered form of the opening track promises an escape from pain through the sublime, then it's not until the grand finale of "Cop Shoot Cop" that we see the natural conclusion of this exploration. The song builds to a climax so intense that it dissolves into a free-jazz noise session, reminding us that the sublime is reached through the sublimation of the self. Here J Spaceman releases himself not just from musical form but also from restraint and identity. It's thrilling but it's also tragic. It reminds us that the drug use glamorized through the rest of the record (the album artwork is even designed to look like pharmaceutical packaging) has a real human price.

So much has been said about this album. That it's a record of J's heartbreak after his girlfriend and Spiritualized co-founder, Kate Radley, eloped with Richard Ashcroft (the album's chilling opening line is supposedly from a kiss-off voicemail she left J Spaceman). That it's the album that introduced suburban white kids to heroin after they heard its euphoric sounds. That it was the perfect marriage of shoegaze and gospel. Nothing says as much to me about this album as that photo of the child, lost in a sea of darkness, navigating only by the symphony of guitars, strings, bells, and the delicate refrain, "All I need in life's a little bit of love to take the pain away/ Getting strong today/A giant step each day."

Like this?
Check out these three too

Beta Band
Champion Versions

Galaxie 500
This Is Our Music

Stereolab
Emperor Tomato Ketchup

DUSTY SPRINGFIELD
DUSTY IN MEMPHIS

by Tom Breihan

On the cover of Dusty Springfield's 1969 album *Dusty in Memphis*, we see the singer, an English lady with a frilly shirt and a beehive hairdo, with both hands smushed up to her face. It's a flirty image, for sure, but the eyes are expressing a universal sentiment: "Oh, shit. What have I gotten myself into?"

Dusty Springfield was not a born soul singer. She didn't have one of those voices. Instead, she was polite, reserved, and poised—quintessentially British, in other words. Through most of the '60s, she'd been one of her homeland's great pop singers. Hers was the sort of graceful, honeyed voice that's right at home singing, say, the Bacharach songbook. But, by the late '60s, that stuff was on the decline. So rather than end up on the oldies circuit, she decided to take advantage of her longtime love of American soul music, signing with Atlantic Records and going to work with Jerry Wexler, the guy who'd invented the phrase "rhythm and blues" and who'd produced classics for Wilson Pickett and Aretha Franklin.

The sessions that produced *Dusty in Memphis* weren't smooth. Springfield got down to Memphis, realized that she'd actually be working with the musicians as they were recording, and decided the whole thing wasn't for her. What we're hearing on *Dusty in Memphis* is actually Dusty in New York, singing over already-finished tracks. And the rollout wasn't smooth, either. The album was a notorious flop; one that pretty much destroyed Springfield's career as a pop force, pushing her toward the margins.

But you don't hear any of those turbulent conditions in *Dusty in Memphis*. Instead, the album is a near-perfect hybrid beast, fusing that sweaty Southern soul with the sort of sweetly crooned pop music Springfield had already made. The album is warm and welcoming and unbelievably pretty, and it's also deeply sexy. (Two of the tracks are about morning fucking.) Aretha Franklin turned down "Son of a Preacher Man," the sole minor hit, and Springfield did it nothing like Franklin would've, making it shy and insinuating. On the rare occasions when she tries out pure vocal firepower, as on the dignified regret anthem, "Don't Forget About Me," she's a force of nature. But, more often, her take on Southern soul is sly and poised and entirely unique.

The whole album stands as one of those moments when everyone involved left their respective comfort zones and found some magical new place. Generations of blue-eyed soul singers would take note.

Like this?
Check out these three too

Wilson Pickett
In the Midnight Hour

Nancy Sinatra
Nancy in London

Ike & Tina Turner
Workin' Together

BRUCE SPRINGSTEEN
NEBRASKA

by Caitlin White

In an era where recording on a tape machine is a quirky, DIY throwback trope, listening to Springsteen's 1982 acoustic album *Nebraska* is a reminder of the raw intimacy this form can bring. Springsteen had already established himself as a monolithic force in the rock world, a firebrand with enough burning personal passion to carry a band on his back—*Nebraska* proved he had the introspection to leave the world just as spellbound with the simplicity of a lone guitar, a harmonica, and an organ. In fact, these songs were all originally intended to be demos that Bruce's E Street Band would later flesh out. It was Springsteen himself who decided the skeletal bedroom recordings were more powerful in their naked and desolate outlines.

While most Springsteen albums center themselves around working-class figures, *Nebraska* is particularly concerned with those who have no hope, the lowest of the low— the musical outlook is as bleak as the view on the cover image. Springsteen's *Nebraska* is populated by doomed mass murderers, and bleak sketches of small-minded criminals, drawn with a peculiar human touch. This is an album steeped in pathos; ordinary and even boring lives full of death and darkness become tender, empathetic odes when they're relayed by the Boss's scratchy, scraggly voice.

"Atlantic City" is one of the few tracks here that covers ground Bruce himself might've called home, and it remains the album's standout. But, damn, if the self-titled opener doesn't sound like it was pulled directly from a cornfield. "Used Cars" is a junkyard heartbreaker about claustrophobic small towns and the tiny dreams that fuel their residents; "Reason to Believe" manages to find a hunk of hope in a landscape littered with roadkill and faithless lovers. Only Springsteen could so deftly hew an album out of the American heartland, remaking manifest destiny in his own image with just a vision and a tape machine. For a better rendition of that precious recording quality, this album will always sound best on vinyl.

Like this?
Check out these three too

Calexico and Iron & Wine In the Reins

Smog Forgotten Foundation

Uncle Tupelo No Depression

Listen to with...

OSKAR'S KEY

Ingredients

1½ fl oz (45ml) rye whiskey

½ fl oz (15ml) St. Elizabeth's
allspice dram

½ fl oz (15ml) fresh lemon juice

½ oz (15g) brown sugar simple syrup

2 dashes of orange bitters

Method

Combine all the ingredients in a
cocktail shaker. Shake well and
strain into an old-fashioned glass.
Top with the orange bitters.

ST. VINCENT
STRANGE MERCY

by Susannah Young

A successful artist writing her third album offers different context for the creative process: you're not announcing yourself or trying to prove you've still got more to say. You're part of the canon, and you've got a captive audience eager to hear what you'll say next. And thus it simultaneously absolves you of all pressure while creating the perfect conditions for creative paralysis.

So it makes sense that in a 2011 interview with Amanda Petrusich, St. Vincent's Annie Clark explained that it was important for her to establish directives for herself when she wrote the songs that would comprise her third album, *Strange Mercy*, saying that defining and enforcing limits was her escape hatch from the terrifying open-endedness of making art—the fastest way to freeze your creative juices. In other words, for Clark, restricting her own movement is a necessary step toward freeing herself to move. The white latex-smothered screaming mouth of the cover art (designed by Clark herself and photographed by Tina Tyrell) could be seen as a visualization of these two contradictory forces.

Movement is written all over *Strange Mercy*. It feels impossible to think about the album without considering it: whether it's better to make a move or stay still, and, if we do make a move, how much *should* we move. All the men and women who comprise *Strange Mercy*'s cast of characters are pointedly framed as stuck, unstuck, or at the electrifying nexus where we decide to *become* unstuck: the sharks circling indecisive Elijah in "Dilettante"; the girl, in "Surgeon," begging for the clean precision of a surgeon's knife to elegantly solve her life; Clark's exorcism of the mental hangover accompanying her year-long battle with deep depression on "Year of the Tiger"; the woman in "Cheerleader" pushing beyond the role others created for her.

Strange Mercy is aggressively, gloriously kinetic, but in a way that's precise, calculated and controlled: a cerebral examination of life's viscera. It doesn't test limits so much as it runs rampant within the boundaries Clark strictly defines for *herself*. This is an artist showing her cards to the table, but doing so one card at a time. Control, release. Control, release.

Like this? Check out these three too

Bat for Lashes
Two Suns

Feist
The Reminder

Perfume Genius
Too Bright

ST. VINCENT

STRANGE MERCY

STEELY DAN
AJA

by Andrew Winistorfer

There's a reason this used to be the album they tested hi-fi audio performance with: four decades since release, it still sounds like a zillion bucks. It's the smoothest of the smooth, the chilliest of the chill.

Aja, Steely Dan's sixth album, is the one that finally melded the group's jazz and classic-pop influences into its own genre. With other jazz-rock albums, you could remove the guitars or the saxophones and be left with either a jazz or a rock album. With *Aja* that's impossible: the jazz flourishes are so ingrained in Steely Dan's perfect sound that they stop being something added for flourish.

Recorded over seven months in 1977, *Aja* features a veritable murderers' row of session musicians, like guitarists Larry Carlton and Jay Graydon, who between them played guitar for basically every pop star from 1975 to 1985, singer Venetta Fields (the Rolling Stones, Pink Floyd), and drummer Jim Keltner, who is famous for working as the drummer for every Beatle but Paul. Big names like Wayne Shorter (the sax solo on the title track), Michael McDonald (backing vocals on "Peg" and "I Got the News"), and the Eagles' Timothy B Schmit ("Aja," "Home at Last," and "Josie")

are broken down to instruments for Steely Dan to use here.

Aja was also Steely Dan's biggest hit, debuting at number three on Billboard, its stark cover art becoming ubiquitous in every dorm room in the late '70s, and selling more than five million copies when it was said and done. Steely Dan were never a "singles band," but the staying power and importance of *Aja* is helped by "Deacon Blues," probably the band's most lasting single, thanks to its lyrics of mid-life crises coming along at the perfect time for the baby boomers who were turning 30 and older in 1977.

Aja came at the end of a mad dash for Steely Dan: their sixth album in six years at the beginning of their career. Their exacting studio techniques, and the demands they put on musicians, engineers, and the two band members Donald Fagen and Walter Becker, led them to taking a 13-year hiatus after 1980's *Gaucho*, and they have only released two albums in the last 35 years. But when you're coming from the peaks and perfection of something as monolithic and well-crafted as *Aja*—even its cover is monumental—taking 35 years to record two albums isn't that unreasonable.

Like this?
Check out these three too

George Benson
Breezin'

Chicago
Chicago II

Michael McDonald
If That's
What It Takes

SUFJAN STEVENS
ILLINOIS

by Tyler Hayes

Illinois—Sufjan Stevens's second state album after *Michigan*—quickly prompted fans to anticipate albums for the other 48 states. At the time, the allure of such a huge undertaking just added to the mythology and intrigue of Stevens as an artist. It takes a unique personality to propose and tease that kind of possibility. Even though the next state album isn't (likely) ever coming—Stevens has said as much—that doesn't stop people from silently hoping against the odds. In the meantime, we're left with a stunning collection of songs (and an award-winning cover by Divya Srinivasan featuring Illinois-related images—Sears Tower, Black Hawk, etc.—as well as the confusing reference to the frequent mispronunciation of the State's name).

As a whole, *Illinois* is the culmination of Stevens's ability to remain a folk singer, and still put out epic anthems overflowing with elaborate narratives. The record is littered with fascinating aspects, both musically and lyrically. And even though "Casimir Pulaski Day" is one of the simpler, softer, and more delicate tracks on the album, it was the first to imminently pierce my heart. More than a track like "Chicago," with upbeat instrumentation, the brutal honesty Stevens seems to have no problem exposing is laid gracefully on top of unassuming guitar, banjo, and horns. "Casimir Pulaski Day" is heartbreaking but also inspirational as the song ramps up at the end and says, without any words, "This life, it's going to be okay."

It's easy to form a theory, but it's hard to explain exactly why *Illinois* works so perfectly as a fairly eclectic collection of songs. Now in the shadows of *Carrie & Lowell*, Stevens's fifth album, there's an attractiveness to the thought that while writing and recording *Illinois* no idea for a song was turned away, but rather all were molded to fit together. This is part of Stevens's charm. The skill to take 22 tracks, all varying in length and temperament, fit them to a theme, and also make the songs work on their own apart from the bunch doesn't come along often.

Like this?
Check out these three too

Beirut
Gulag Orkestar

The Decemberists
Picaresque

The Shins
Chutes Too Narrow

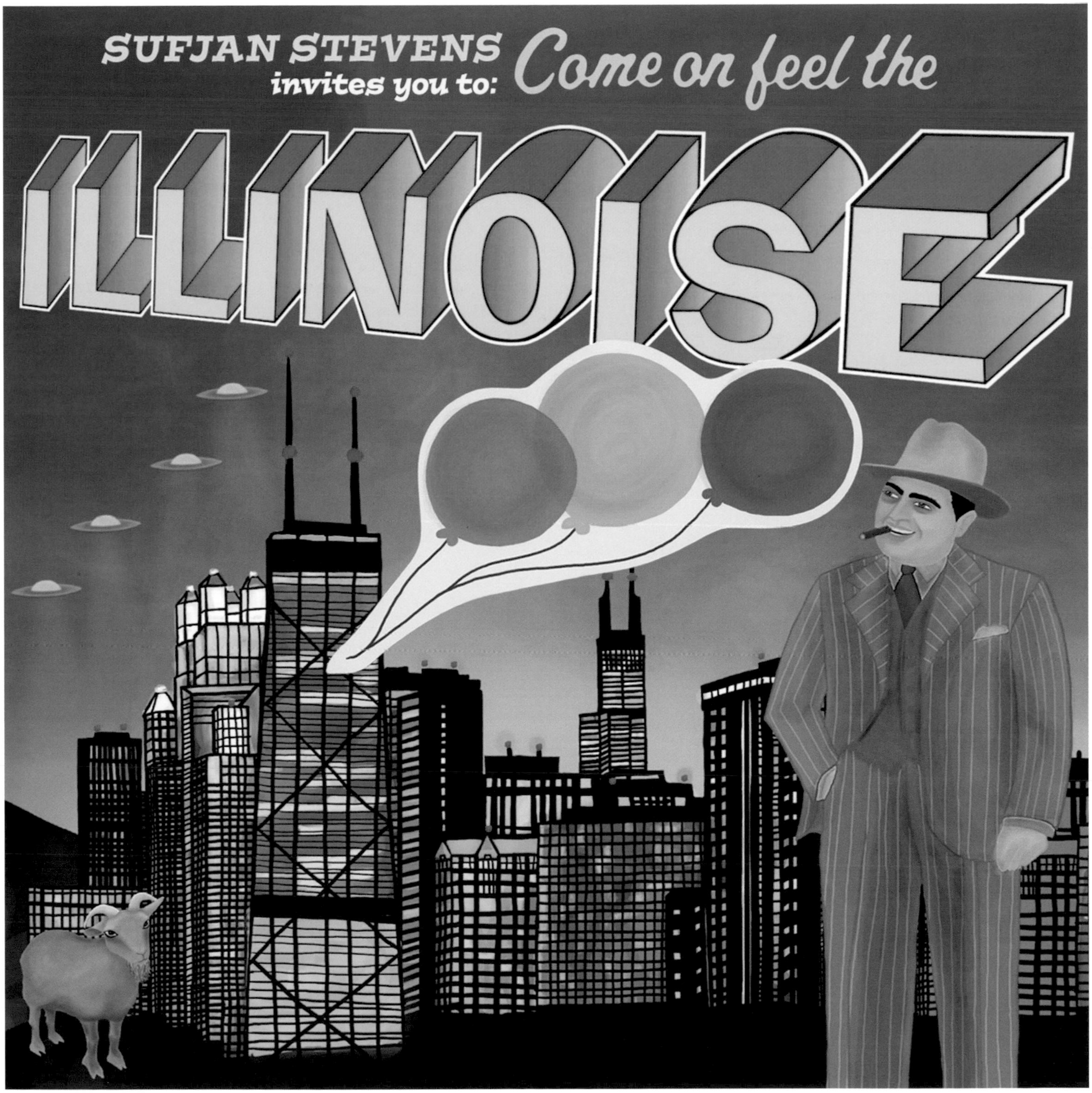
SUFJAN STEVENS
invites you to:
Come on feel the
ILLINOISE

THE STROKES IS THIS IT

THE STROKES
IS THIS IT

by Eric Sundermann

When the Strokes burst onto the scene in the early 2000s, they came to represent everything we have always wanted and will always want out of rock 'n' roll. Youthful. Charming. Cocky. Cool. Each member of the band—especially frontman Julian Casablancas—seemed to take every cliché that's ever existed about what it means to sing songs with guitars and embrace it. They wore leather jackets. Their tight jeans had holes in them. Their haircuts looked expensively shitty. Somehow, nothing about them felt like an act or like they were patronizing (even though they probably were). Instead, it worked because, at the time, we didn't just want it—we fucking needed it.

Is This It released in 2001, the heyday of garbage post-grunge rock music made by the likes of Creed and a bunch of other bands that sounded like Creed (you know, the ones with singers who sound like they're gargling salt water while they sing vague lyrics that don't really mean anything). Is it extreme to say that this album saved us? Probably. But, on the other hand, it really did.

Even before the record released, the band was steaming with hype, gaining buzz, especially in the New York City scene, as they moved from stalwarts at clubs on Avenue A to photo spreads in magazines—back when photo spreads in magazines were still a really big deal. People wanted them, and they knew it, which somehow made their sexiness even more appealing. Hell, even the title of the record, the casual dismissiveness (that doesn't bother including a question mark) of its tone stayed true to how damn cool these cats were—never mind the obligatory ruffling of feathers caused by the now-legendary image of the naked backside on the album's cover.

No other group could've taken the jangling glory of '70s punk and brought it into the new century. With songs like "Barely Legal," "Take It or Leave It," and "Last Nite," the Strokes embraced the simple stupidity of youth, that time period in your life when you don't just think you'll live forever, you know it.

Like this? Check out these three too

Interpol
Antics

Kings of Leon
Aha Shake Heartbreak

Yeah Yeah Yeahs
Fever to Tell

SUICIDE
SUICIDE

by Geoff Rickly

Punk started in New York City and don't let anyone tell you otherwise. Years before the Ramones, Suicide coined the term "punk" to describe their antagonistic, at times violent performances (first at the Mercer Arts Center, later at CBGB's). By the time the two-piece ensemble of Martin Rev and Alan Vega released 1977's *Suicide*, the record instead documented their musical movement into an evocative minimalist style that prefigured post-punk, predicted the rise of electronic music, and prophesied the death of rock 'n' roll, all at once, from the music down to its smeared, violent cover.

Opener "Ghost Rider" rolls in on a fiery bass line like the furious comic vigilante it's named after, raising hell with sharp keyboards and Alan Vega's voice set nervously between rock incantations and manic whoops. The sleazy production and detached vocals would provide influence for everyone from Big Black through Joy Division to Nine Inch Nails, and set out a veritable blueprint for later bands like the Faint.

If "Ghost Rider" presaged the post-punk revolution, "Cheree" similarly provided a starting point for Spacemen 3 to take woozy organs and twinkling ruminations to unimaginable, drugged-out heights. Almost a lullaby, with Vega's crooned "Cheree, Cheree/ Oh, baby," it has one of the sweeter melodies and atmospheres of any entry in the punk canon. This was always one of the essential strengths of Rev and Vega's work together: they were able to imagine new genres without feeling indebted to them.

"Frankie Teardrop" is near mythical in the annals of music. The rushing urgency of the 16-on-the-floor drum-machine beat has twice the speed of anything the Sex Pistols would ever set to tape, and the manic screams of Alan Vega, midway through this 10-minute marathon, scrape the paint off the Detroit-built recordings of its nearest relative, the MC5. If punk owes a debt to their musical direction, Kanye and Pusha T must bow to the echoed screams that pulse on "Ghost Rider" and reach apocalyptic heights on "Frankie Teardrop."

Subsequent deluxe versions of *Suicide* would provide context in the form of "23 Minutes Over Brussels" and "96 Tears (Live at CBGB's)." The latter, a cover of Question Mark & the Mysterians' classic, is a brief glimpse into who Rev and Vega looked to for influence. In the end, the original release carries all you need to know about the violence and tenderness of a band that could convincingly sing, "Cheree, Cheree/ Oh, baby/Oh, baby/I love you," and, "We're all Frankies/We're all lying in hell" on the same album.

Like this? Check out these three too

Wire
Pink Flag

Various Artists
No New York

The Velvet
Underground
White Light/
White Heat

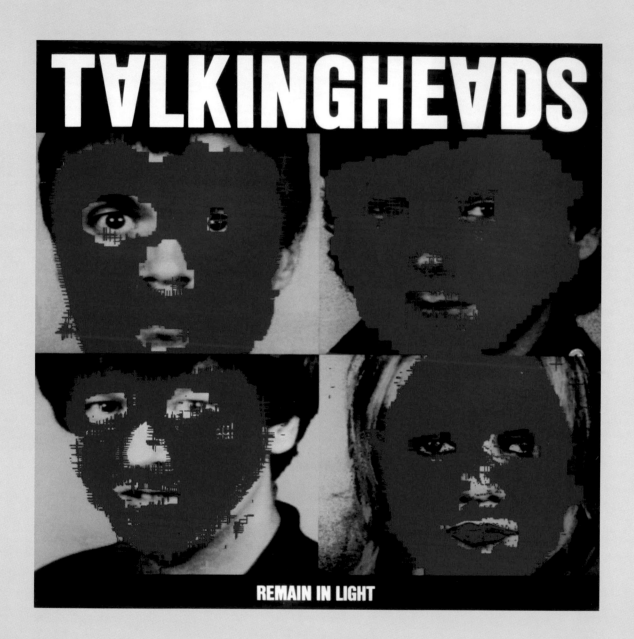

TALKING HEADS
REMAIN IN LIGHT

by Caitlin White

Remain in Light was released on the cusp of the '80s, a glittering portent of a decade full of suspicion and hair metal. African polyrhythms and glitchy synthesizers come courtesy of Brian Eno and funk; the prophetic babbling of David Byrne comes courtesy of Talking Heads, who were spending this album attempting to prove Byrne wasn't outshining the rest of the band.

Instead, he and Eno outdid the group so thoroughly that they both became marquee names long after another decade of internal strife drove the band asunder (bassist Tina Weymouth allegedly considered putting Eno's face over the band's portraits on the cover of *Remain in Light*, to reflect what she viewed as his egotism). Still, the impact of keyboardist Jerry Harrison, and husband-and-wife duo drummer Chris Frantz and Weymouth were critical components in the construction of this uneasy, shrieking art-pop masterpiece.

Byrne babbles and flashes with the intensity of a street preacher, inspired by and liberally borrowing from the elocution of a pulpit-pounder on everything from "Once in a Lifetime" to "Crosseyed and Painless," and even album-opener "Born Under Punches (The Heat Goes On)." Of course, his random, blocky bundles of phrasing only worked so well in contrast to the flailing funk and oddball samples that Eno helped the band incorporate into their sound.

At times the album is dystopian and minimalist, before launching into long, drawn-out jams or breathless, brilliant bursts of unrelenting groove. It's difficult to find any sort of companion piece or comparable touchstone to this album; much like Byrne or Eno, it stands apart on a plane all its own, a testament to the singular vision of these two artists. Don't miss a single iota of their supercharged funk frisson—listen to the damn thing on a real sound system.

Like this?
Check out these three too

The B-52's
Cosmic Thing

Elvis Costello and the Attractions
Punch the Clock

Devo
Freedom of Choice

THIN LIZZY
JAILBREAK

by Andrew Winistorfer

Is there a more quintessentially America-in-the-1970s album than *Jailbreak*? It's an album full of street toughs, bleary-eyed drunkards coming to terms with life not going like they thought it would, cowboys, Romeos, and those chicks who got up and slapped Johnny's face. It sounds like the American Bicentennial, it sounds like 30 hot dogs on a grill, it sounds like muscle cars on hot asphalt, and it sounds like the first 15 minutes of *The Warriors* (as a side note: artist Jim Fitzpatrick and Phil Lynott came up with the concept of "The Warrior" for the album's artwork—influenced by Marvel comics and Wells's *War of the Worlds*).

Bruce Springsteen and John Mellencamp get all the credit for making music working-class Americans allegedly wanted and needed to hear in the late '70s, but *Jailbreak* came the closest to giving the working class the soundtrack of their actual lives in 1976. That it was made by a band of Irishmen with a black lead singer makes that achievement even more unlikely.

Recorded in late 1975 under pressure from their record company to record a hit album—their previous five albums had mostly stalled out before entering the British album charts, and had never even sniffed American charts—Thin Lizzy wrote the defining album of their career. Buoyed by the swinging, interlocking,

open-hearted guitar tones and solos of Brian Robertson and Scott Gorham, and the workaday poetry of Phil Lynott, *Jailbreak* is one of the best guitar albums of the '70s and beyond.

Everyone knows the rightfully canonical singles—"Jailbreak," "Cowboy Song," and "The Boys Are Back in Town," which is still the best song about getting loaded with your friends—but *Jailbreak*'s first single was actually "Running Back," the lost classic of the album. "I make my money singing songs about you/It's my claim to fame," Lynott sings to an ex here, aware that he's all bluster before admitting he'd go running back if she asked. There are more hidden gems: "Fight or Fall" is the most tender Thin Lizzy song, and "Romeo and the Lonely Girl" is one of Lynott's finest overwrought guitar poems, all Big Themes and Big Riffs.

Jailbreak broke Thin Lizzy beyond just the UK: it was their first gold album in the US. But it was also their only one; they never became the powerhouse they could have, partially due to later releases doubling down on the metal, and partially because Lynott caught hepatitis on the US tour for *Jailbreak* and later succumbed to heroin addiction. But they live on in infamy, along with the rest of the guys immortalized on "The Boys Are Back in Town."

Like this?
Check out these three too

AC/DC
Highway to Hell

Aerosmith
Rocks

Nazareth
Hair of the Dog

JAILBREAK · THIN LIZZY
VERTIGO
RED ALERT.
JAILBREAK!
JIM FITZPATRICK · 76

JUSTIN TIMBERLAKE
FUTURESEX/LOVESOUNDS

by Drew Millard

By 2006, the world had known Justin Timberlake for a decade. They knew his work with the boy band NSYNC, they knew his beautiful falsetto, they knew his impeccable dance moves, they knew his solo hits "Rock Your Body," "Señorita," and "Cry Me a River." But the world wanted—nay, *needed*—to know one thing: Did Justin Timberlake fuck?

The answer, delivered in the form of *FutureSex/LoveSounds*, was a resounding yes. Justin Timberlake did in fact fuck.

Its Terry Richardson–shot cover image—featuring Timberlake in a natty suit stomping a disco ball to death—doubled as a statement of purpose. *FutureSex/LoveSounds* is one of those records so sonically divorced from the context of the pop music around it that it will never not sound like it was beamed down from another dimension. Though the album took inspiration from the trance, crunk, and indie rock of its time, it was all filtered through a bizarro analog-future vision of Timberlake, producer Timbaland, and his right-hand man Nate "Danja" Hills. The record opens with what can best be described as the Transylvanian disco-funk of "FutureSex/LoveSound" and "SexyBack," which is easily the strangest song of the 2000s

to hit number one on the Billboard Hot 100. Then there's "My Love," inescapable and transcendent in its declarations of total and unwavering commitment; then the swirling, nervy "LoveStoned," which flips halfway through and morphs unexpectedly into "I Think She Knows," perhaps an even finer faux-indie-rock track than Kelly Clarkson's "Since U Been Gone." The record is full of such push-and-pull between randy come-ons and unexpected asides, whether it's inviting Timberlake's fellow Tennesseans Three 6 Mafia to come roam in the sandbox that is "Chop Me Up," or the Lynchian middle school dance ballad "(Another Song) All Over Again."

It's hard to understate the impact that *FutureSex/LoveSounds* had after its release. The record was inescapable, spawning six hit singles and a massive stadium tour. More than that, it vaunted Timberlake into the echelon of the pop greats such as Michael Jackson and Prince—Timberlake, Timbaland, and Danja understood that if you wanted to make your generation's *Thriller* or *Purple Rain*, you couldn't try to replicate the sounds of *Thriller* and *Purple Rain*—you needed to create an entirely new flavor of funk altogether.

Like this?
Check out these three too

Justin Bieber
Purpose

Michael Jackson
Thriller

Usher
My Way

A TRIBE CALLED QUEST
MIDNIGHT MARAUDERS

by Ben Munson

A Tribe Called Quest's classic *Midnight Marauders* cover almost didn't happen. According to a smoking-section interview with Jive Records art director Nick Gamma, the cover was not Q-Tip's first choice. He originally wanted to feature a woman listening to music in headphones while touching herself. If not that, he wanted the striped woman with headphone jacks coming out of her head, leading a group of people wearing the same pair of giant headphones past the Flatiron Building. One idea got nixed because of the masturbatory implications, and the other because it was too difficult to do with the available technology at the time. Instead, the group went with pictures of every rapper and DJ that could show up for separate photo shoots in New York City and Los Angeles.

As it stands, the portraits of hip-hop heads that appear on Tribe's third full-length act as a document of rap culture around the time of its 1993 release. Depending on whether the clock frame is green, red, or black, anyone from breaker Mr. Wiggles to Kool DJ Red Alert to Diddy might show up on the front. It's basically everyone except Q-Tip, Phife Dawg, Ali Shaheed Muhammad, and Jarobi White.

Most of the other classic hip-hop albums that touched down in 1993—including indelible debuts from the Wu-Tang Clan and Digable Planets—put the artists front and center. Tribe didn't need their images on the cover to give listeners a clear picture of who they were. Across its nearly one-hour running time, Q-Tip and Phife take care to pack their lyrics with well-crafted warnings to question their skills while also turning in the mostly tightly produced and accessible music of Tribe's incredible three-album run.

Midnight Marauders coalesced the jazz rap of *The Low End Theory* and the story-form raps of *People's Instinctive Travels and the Paths of Rhythm* into a less rambling, funkier whole. Phife's inventory of stress on "8 Million Stories" is matched with a crunchy vertigo beat. "Electric Relaxation" astroglides across wavy smoothness as Q-Tip and Phife trade lusty couplets. But the bulk of *Midnight Marauders* plays like boast rap. Starting with "Award Tour," the group lets it be known that they deserve this career highlight, and that those who would oppose them don't deserve to breathe the same air. It's an occasion to sit back and give the album cover spotlight to someone else.

Like this?
Check out these three too

Digable Planets
Blowout Comb

Jungle Brothers
Straight Out the Jungle

The Pharcyde
Bizarre Ride II The Pharcyde

TV ON THE RADIO
RETURN TO COOKIE MOUNTAIN

by Andrew Winistorfer

The story of indie rock in the 2000s is how quickly major labels went from being dismissive of the bands of Brooklynites, who were lighting up sites like *Pitchfork*, to trying to sign those very bands to record deals. If no record was going to sell more than 300,000 copies, the majors figured, might as well sign bands that will top out at that number. You had bands like Black Kids, the Decemberists, and Interpol get snatched out of indie stardom to be bankrolled by major-label suits.

Even with the indie-rock gold rush, there wasn't a more unlikely band for major-label pickup than TV on the Radio—the group of five art-rock weirdos who seemed to draw inspiration from drum circles, David Bowie's Berlin trilogy, someone yelling out music from the bottom of a well, and electrocution. Thanks to cosigns from everyone from *Pitchfork* to Bowie* himself for their debut LP (*Desperate Youth, Blood Thirsty Babes*), TV on the Radio found themselves signed to Interscope, Jimmy Iovine's predominantly gangsta-rap label. But the deal seemed perfect: they basically gave TV on the Radio money to go away and record albums every two years.

The first of these is the group's finest, *Return to Cookie Mountain*, arguably the peak moment for indie rock in the 2000s. Built around Tunde Adebimpe and Kyp Malone's harrowed, howling, and haunted vocals, and Dave Sitek's claustrophobic production and layered guitar work, *Return* is like a score for a movie about killing a great beast in a swamp. "Wolf Like Me" is the song that became the nominal "hit," but you could take any of the 11 and put them on your indie-rock mixtape and they'd steal the show.

Picking the "best" moments here is an exercise in minutiae. The way the guitars chime over Adebimpe's vocals on "Tonight"; the way you can only hear Bowie's voice on "Province" if you have good headphones, then he's impossible to miss; the feeling you get in your chest when the drums drop on "A Method"; how the riff of "Playhouses" feels like being repeatedly pummeled by waves.

TV on the Radio have released three albums since this, but none is such a widescreen success, with minor flourishes that make it as consistently rewarding.

*Like Bowie, Tunde Adebimpe and David Andrew Sitek are visual artists—Adebimpe's work graces the cover of *Return to Cookie Mountain*: an abandoned bird's nest, which echoes a crown of thorns.

Like this?
Check out these three too

David Bowie
Low

Menomena
Friend and Foe

Yeasayer
All Hour Cymbals

UGK
RIDIN' DIRTY

by Drew Millard

From the opening notes of the Mr. 3-2-featuring "One Day" to the easy wah-wah guitars of the album's shout-out outro, *Ridin' Dirty* set the template for dirty South-country rap tunes. Though UGK already had two albums (*Too Hard to Swallow, Super Tight*) and a handful of regional anthems ("Playaz from the South," "Pocket Full of Stones," "Front, Back & Side to Side") under their candy-painted belts, it wasn't until *Ridin' Dirty* that the Underground Kingz delivered their definitive statement of Southern excellence.

Ridin' Dirty was recorded in a time of great strife for UGK. They'd just parted ways with a duplicitous manager and blown most of their advance recording an album in Chicago that was so bad that even Pimp C's own mother told them it sucked. So, they packed up for their hometown of Houston, Texas, ridin' dirty like on the cover, to re-do the record. But at home friends were dying and getting arrested, while Pimp C was embroiled in a custody battle over his child. The duo put every ounce of the pain and hardship around them into the record, bringing in live instrumentation and vocals when they couldn't afford sample clearances, and sneaking their incarcerated compatriot Smoke D a voice recorder in jail so that he might deliver dispatches live from the front lines of the drug war. Bun B—never a slouch on the mic—had developed into one of the most astute and literary spitters below the Mason-Dixon line, while Pimp C switched between soulful singing and his unique, slurred rap style, full of colloquialisms so Southern they could have come out a deep frier.

Pimp C was once quoted as saying that when he and Bun B made music as UGK, the results weren't quite hip-hop or rap, but instead "real n**** blues." And that's a great way to look at their 1996 masterpiece *Ridin' Dirty*—as the greatest rapped blues album ever.

Like this?
Check out these three too

**Geto Boys
We Can't
Be Stopped**

**Slim Thug
Already
Platinum**

**Three 6 Mafia
Mystic Stylez**

Townes Van Zandt

Live at The Old Quarter, Houston, Texas

TOWNES VAN ZANDT
LIVE AT THE OLD QUARTER, HOUSTON, TEXAS

by Luke Winkie

It was supposedly a sweltering week at the Old Quarter in the summer of 1973. The unadorned brick walls of the Houston club stood still, 11 by 38, packed to the gills with just over 100 paying customers. No air conditioning, no seating, a small set of restrooms upstairs; if that sounds like a hellscape, well, you're not far off.

"Cooling refreshments were hard to come by, requiring the passing of the money up through many hands to the bar, and an arduous return trip of the foamy mugs back through the same hands," wrote producer Earl Willis in the liner notes. "If you know Houston in July, then you have an idea how hot and humid it was in that room, and leaving the door open did little good except, perhaps, to improve the clarity of the sound of passing buses from the nearby bus station."

But somehow, through all the stickiness and saltiness, all the drunken inconvenience that comes with your usual live-music experience, the crowd is absolutely absorbed for all 92 minutes of *Live at the Old Quarter*. Townes Van Zandt and his guitar, alone, untethered, his pure North Texas dryness carving out his spot in history. Zandt was already six albums deep in a legendary career, but this was one of those nights. A particularly heartfelt take on the vagabond tale "Pancho and Lefty" decimates the room; not a cough, or a whisper, or a dropped beer, and Zandt can hardly believe it himself. "I've never heard it so quiet in here," he remarks, after the applause.

Live music sucks. It's expensive, uncomfortable, and futile. The bands are exhausted; the set list is too long; gentle murmurs from the bar cut through songs that sound better on record anyway. But you keep going, because occasionally something magical happens. *Live at the Old Quarter* is one of the most reassuring albums ever made. Sometimes, even in the dank Houston humidity, the stars align, and magic exists.

Like this? Check out these three too

Steve Earle
Guitar Town

Emmylou Harris
Blue Kentucky Girl

Gram Parsons
Grievous Angel

TOM WAITS
BONE MACHINE

by Chris Lay

Upon its release, Tom Waits's 11th album, 1992's *Bone Machine*, was many things all at once. It marked a rebirth, with Waits breaking a five-year stretch of studio-album silence, but it's also an album that personifies the sensation of someone walking over your grave. With songs like "Jesus Gonna Be Here," "Earth Died Screaming," "Dirt in the Ground," and "The Ocean Doesn't Want Me," *Bone Machine* finds Waits playing with all sorts of existential endings, from homicide and suicide, scaling all the way up to the literal matricidal death of mother earth itself. Jesse Dylan's photo of Waits on the artwork captures something of this apocalyptic vision: a seemingly screaming Waits, leather skull-capped and sporting protective goggles. It's not all doom and gloom, though, since it also gives us "Goin' Out West," which, with its chorus of "I look good without a shirt," sadly has a few chest hairs too many to be the dead-end strip-club anthem it deserves to be.

Preceded by, and arguably lost in the wake of, the so-called "Island trilogy" of *Swordfishtrombones*, *Rain Dogs*, and *Franks Wild Years*, *Bone Machine* pulls off the difficult task of synthesizing the best elements of those albums under one cover while simultaneously taking a huge step toward the more mature elder-statesman persona that would get more flesh on its bones by the time 1999's *Mule Variations* rolled around. Don't get me wrong: you still get the German dwarfs and the references to rusted-out carnival rides, but there's just a bit more meat filling in the cracks here.

The album works a little better when you assume all the percussive elements come from human bones clacking around. Sure, it's not true, but that it's even within the realm of overall believability speaks volumes for why this album above all his others is Waits's best. *Bone Machine* does feature one of the most outlandish instruments ever concocted, the "conundrum," which you can hear in action on "In the Colosseum." Designed by Waits's sculptor neighbor, it's an iron cross with metal elements hanging off it that are meant to be hit (hard) with a hammer. Waits says the conundrum *looks* like a Chinese torture device, *sounds* like a jail door closing, and *feels* therapeutic, which goes a long way to summing up the overarching vibe of this album. Growth, both inward and outward.

Like this?
Check out these three too

Nick Cave and the Bad Seeds
Let Love In

Primus
Pork Soda

Warren Zevon
Excitable Boy

ROOT OF ALL EVIL

Ingredients

2 fl oz (60ml) bourbon

½ fl oz (15ml) Cointreau

½ fl oz (15ml) Fernet-Branca

¼ fl oz (10ml) maraschino liqueur

2 dashes of orange bitters

ice

orange peel, to garnish

Method

Half fill a cocktail shaker with ice and
add all the ingredients except the orange
peel. Shake vigorously to combine,
then strain into a chilled cocktail glass.
Garnish with orange peel and serve.

THE WAR ON DRUGS LOST IN THE DREAM

THE WAR ON DRUGS
LOST IN THE DREAM

by Tyler Barstow

I'm one of the people who thinks *Lost in the Dream* was the best album of 2014, and I figured I would get that out on the table now. I think that because it was, but we don't need to fight about it now. For those unfamiliar, the War on Drugs was founded in 2005 by a guy named Adam Granduciel and another guy named Kurt Vile. Vile left, with no hard feelings on either side, after their debut *Wagonwheel Blues* was released in 2008, to start a solo career you might have heard a thing or two about, and left Adam and Co. to carry on the good fight without him. And carry it on they certainly did, releasing the very good *Slave Ambient* in 2011 and this objectively better follow-up in 2014.

There are the obvious comparisons to Dylan and Springsteen here, and those are deserved. Lines like "And I don't mind you disappearing/When I know you can be found/When you living on the dark side of the street, damn/We're just living in the moment, making our past/Losin' our grasp through the grand parade" don't exist in a vacuum. But to call this album an homage of any kind is to miss the point. This thing is part empty-highway hymn book and part punching through the clouds. Part long walk into paradise and part long walk back out. It's Adam Granduciel singing his way through the pre-dawn dark as best he can and letting us listen while he does. It's cinematic, and haunted, and full of the kind of unironic pain that shares a last name with love.

This is the kind of album your dad might say they don't make anymore, except they do, and they did. Depending on your age, it carries itself like an album that came out when you were a kid. And there's so much to learn from it that the only real way to engage with it is to set aside an evening to spin it three or four times in a row and let it speak for itself. It's ragged, it's resigned, and in so many different ways it's earned its place on any record shelf.

Like this?
Check out these three too

Real Estate
Days

Kurt Vile
b'lieve i'm goin down...

The Walkmen
Bows + Arrows

THE NEWARK

Ingredients

2 fl oz (60ml) Laird's bonded apple brandy

1 fl oz (30ml) Vya sweet vermouth

¼ fl oz (10ml) Fernet-Branca

¼ fl oz (10ml) maraschino liqueur

ice

Method

Combine all the ingredients in a mixing glass
and stir. Strain into a chilled coupe glass.

Notes

Recipe courtesy of Joe Day

KAMASI WASHINGTON
THE EPIC

by Gary Suarez

To what do we owe the coronation of the 21st century's first genuine jazz star? Some would credit Kamasi Washington's ascent to Kendrick Lamar, the West Coast rap savior whose Grammy-winning *To Pimp a Butterfly* album prominently featured the saxophonist's work. Others might cite Flying Lotus, the tastemaking producer and forward-thinking independent-label operator, whose shrewd stewardship allowed a relative unknown the opportunity to release some three hours of mostly original compositions.

Yet whatever person or cosmic force made this happen, it is important not to let that diminish the actual work of Washington and his formidable band of musicians that performed on *The Epic*—an appropriate title for a triple album. Some of those on the record have been playing in one way or another alongside him for well over a decade. Fellow Los Angelenos Ronald Bruner Jr., Stephen "Thundercat" Bruner, and Cameron Graves were all with Washington in the Young Jazz Giants quartet back in 2004.

Perhaps that's why he seems so comfortable in these tunes.

Opener "Change of the Guard" gives *The Epic* a jubilant start, while "Miss Understanding" raises the tempo and with little more than a percussive flutter. A soul-stirring rendition of Ray Noble's standard "Cherokee" comes with Patrice Quinn's lilting pipes at the fore. On the bold "Malcolm's Theme," the band initially treads lightly as it duets with the confident and controlled Dwight Trible, though that soon gives way to a grand solo and eventually a powerful speech from the departed leader referenced in its title.

Collectors should note the deluxe three-LP vinyl edition is a striking package, worthy of speedy purchase and prominent display. The cover image is a star-dusted invitation into Washington's universe, which is hard to resist. The danger, of course, is that the attractive box and lengthy runtime could make *The Epic* a sort of curio. It deserves better than that lazy fate. It deserves attention, attentiveness, and applause.

Like this?
Check out these three too

John Coltrane
Sun Ship

Herbie Hancock
Head Hunters

Kendrick Lamar
To Pimp a Butterfly

KANYE WEST
808s & HEARTBREAK

by Caitlin White

Critics in particular take a certain kind of glee in an album like *808s & Heartbreak*, where the consensus about its worth changed rapidly from flop to flawless. When Kanye abandoned his claim to the rap throne and began gunning for a position as a prominent musician and *artist* outside of the term rapper, no one really took him seriously. And when he proceeded to make an entire album in 2008 about his anguish, cloaked in the icy and immaculate force of Auto-Tune, people were downright scornful. But, at least in the current climate and for the foreseeable future, *808s & Heartbreak* is regarded as a premonition; the album so clearly indicates the way West continually steers the course of popular music, flying one step ahead of the Zeitgeist.

The record is famously about the worst year in West's life—the deflated heart shot by Kristen Yiengst and designed by Virgil Abloh is no red herring: he broke up with his fiancée and blamed his own focus on celebrity for the tragic death of his mother, who passed away unexpectedly during a routine cosmetic surgery. His ability to span the entirety of the emotional spectrum with unrelenting maximalism is truly the core of his triumph. "Heartless" remains one of the greatest odes to the toxic breakup/makeup pattern most of us have experienced at one point, and "Street Lights" is a synthy, star-gazing lullaby worthy of the Phil Collins references West invoked in the making of this album.

But as is the case with most Kanye albums, it's the more gleeful, campy moments that make *808s* so lovable; the Stephen King allusions on "RoboCop," or the way he smiles compassion through his warped vocals for an insecure lover on "Paranoid." These moments find counterparts in the fluttering and booming drums of despair on "Coldest Winter" and the jittery, bass-driven "Love Lockdown," and, yes, the album is more sullen and dejected than any others in Yeezy's catalog. But to hear those off-the-cuff laughs and adlibs on "Paranoid" is to hear a genius in the making, grinning at his own future success, critics be damned.

Like this?
Check out these three too

Bon Iver
For Emma, Forever Ago

Drake
Take Care

Kid Cudi
Man on the Moon: The End of Day

THE WHITE STRIPES
ELEPHANT

by Chris Lay

The White Stripes always wanted to be a Big band, with a capital B. Their third album, 2001's *White Blood Cells*, rode the garage-revival wave into our collective awareness, and there were two albums just as good that had come before it for their newfound national fan base to discover and fall in love with over the nearly two years between that and the giant leap forward that would be *Elephant*.

More than the albums that preceded it, *Elephant* has the sort of confident swagger that will steal your date. They only sent out vinyl copies of the album to reviewers "because if a journalist or a critic doesn't own a record player, I don't really trust them," Jack White explained. The vinyl artwork also threw out a challenge: stare at it long enough, and according to White, you'll see more than one outline of an elephant.

None of this matters, though, if the music isn't on point, and pound for pound, side by duo-chromatic side, almost inarguably *Elephant* still stands as the band's masterwork. The Viking drums of "Seven Nation Army" kick the door in straight off, calling forth the hounds of hell both sonically and literally. The skritchity-scratch guitar throb of "Black Math" hot on its heels, and the one-two-three punch of the first side wraps up with the bittersweet kiss-off "There's No Home for You Here."

Side two opens with "I Just Don't Know What to Do with Myself," which is, of all things, a beefed-up Burt Bacharach cover, before slowing things down and giving Meg White a place to shine with the plaintive request for some winter warmth, "In the Cold, Cold Night." From there, Jack takes the reigns and melts some country slide guitar over the piano-driven "I Want to Be the Boy to Warm Your Mother's Heart," and then the side wraps up with "You've Got Her in Your Pocket," which manages to rhyme "pocket" and "locket," and somehow not sound silly. All that manic magic from the fella who might possibly "be your third man, girl," and you still have the second half of the album to come!

Like this?
Check out these three too

The Kills
Midnight Boom

Led Zeppelin
IV

Son House
Father of
Folk Blues

yankee hotel foxtrot / wilco

WILCO
YANKEE HOTEL FOXTROT

by Susannah Young

We are hardwired to give and receive stories: this is part of the bedrock of human connection, the thing that never changes about the way we reach out to one another, even as the *ways* we're able to reach out change profoundly. Something so ingrained in our needs and so fundamental to our sense of emotional well-being and our ability to trust others should be easy for us to do, but we're not always responsible or kind with one another's stories—and so our accumulated life experience inevitably pushes us to a point where we're dying to reach out to someone but feel too vulnerable, unsafe, and afraid to do so wholly and honestly.

Yankee Hotel Foxtrot chronicles that desperate push/pull between baring all and putting up barriers—and the album itself sprang from the same circumstances it depicts. These songs were born out of misunderstanding, arguing, anger, and sickness: from Jeff Tweedy's horrific migraines, and the addiction they spawned, to the fights with Jay Bennett while recording the album, uncomfortably chronicled in *I Am Trying to Break Your Heart*. They're songs about difficult people made by difficult people for difficult people.

Yankee Hotel Foxtrot also reached us at a difficult time. The album straddles the gap between the Music Industry As It Once Was and the Music Industry We Know Today.

Warner Music Group wouldn't release the album because the company wasn't willing to take a risk on the band's flirtation with art rock—and Wilco responded by doing something that's now par for the course: taking control of their own music and streaming the album online on its original release date. *Yankee Hotel Foxtrot* straddles another gap: the one between pre- and post-9/11 America. These songs about people groping through the fog of anxiety, boredom, paranoia, alienation, and dissatisfaction reached American ears eight days after 9/11. We were needing, willing, and ready to receive those stories—stories that illuminate the most uncomfortable truth about human connection in the modern world*: even with so many outlets to make ourselves known to anyone, everyone feels misunderstood.

Yet in creating an album showing us at our most evasive, Wilco connected with an entire generation. How fitting and ironic that the album title references the NATO phonetic alphabet, an entire system of communication designed to eliminate confusion, to leave no room for error.

*It is interesting that for the artwork of the album, the band chose an image of the towers of Chicago's Marina City, whose architect declared that, in their design, he was "revolting against the idea of man made in the image of the machine"—fulfilling a desire to bring architecture back onto a more human footing.

Like this?
Check out these three too

My Morning Jacket
Z

The National
Boxer

Radiohead
OK Computer

THE XX
XX

by Geoff Rickly

The xx were unlikely candidates to perfectly capture the sound of intimacy on record. Brits, after all, are famous for their icy emotional reserve. Compound that with the fact that the members of the xx were teens, barely out of high school, and you probably wouldn't expect them to produce a lovesick masterpiece of unmatched subtlety, nuance, and feeling. But on their 2009 debut, *xx*, that's just what they did.

The album starts with the effervescent sugar rush of young love on "Intro," thanks in no small part to producer Jamie Smith, who would soon become Jamie xx and deliver one of the most well-loved electronic records of modern times with *In Colour*. Here the production crackles with excitement. Slamming hip-hop drums worthy of a Rihanna song (she in fact sampled it for "Drunk on Love") give way to bright guitar steel pans and group vocals, buzzing over the top like a secret too good to share. The simplicity of the song is immediately evident, and it positively soars. "VCR" and "Crystalised" solidify the formula of club-worthy beats accompanied by taut rolling bass lines and percussive guitars by adding the call-and-answer vocals of Romy Madley Croft and Oliver Sim.

If this formula held up over the length of the album, it would still be an impressive trick. On these early songs the xx use an understated command of their instruments and a brave assertion of minimalism to evoke the simple pleasures: the tropical breeze, the careless touch, the playful give and take of a lover's discourse. On "Crystalised" you sense the closeness of the players. The decision to record live in the tiny XL studio only furthers the impression of the young band swaying together to the beat as it slows to a crawl at the song's conclusion.

The album, however, takes a massive turn at the start of side B. On "Fantasy" the small pleasures melt away in a haze. By "Shelter" the breezy minimalism expands into something grand. The xx's craft becomes architectural. Where before you could hear them swaying together, now you can sense them breathing together. The rumble of the drums become far-off thunder. Their longing could fill an airplane hangar as they evoke unrequited love, sleeplessness, the bitter give and take of exes fighting. Anyone underestimating them had to consider their mistake. Suddenly even the band's name became a multidimensional statement: the sculpturally perfect identical Xs doubled as the informal greeting of two kisses and then redoubled as "the exes." This could be the young band's thesis. That simple things hold multitudes. That simplicity can be deceptive, and that love is a self-contained thing, carrying with it its own sweet beginning, long mysterious middle, and bitter end.

Like this? Check out these three too

Chromatics
Kill for Love

Cold Specks
I Predict a Graceful Expulsion

Young Marble Giants
Colossal Youth

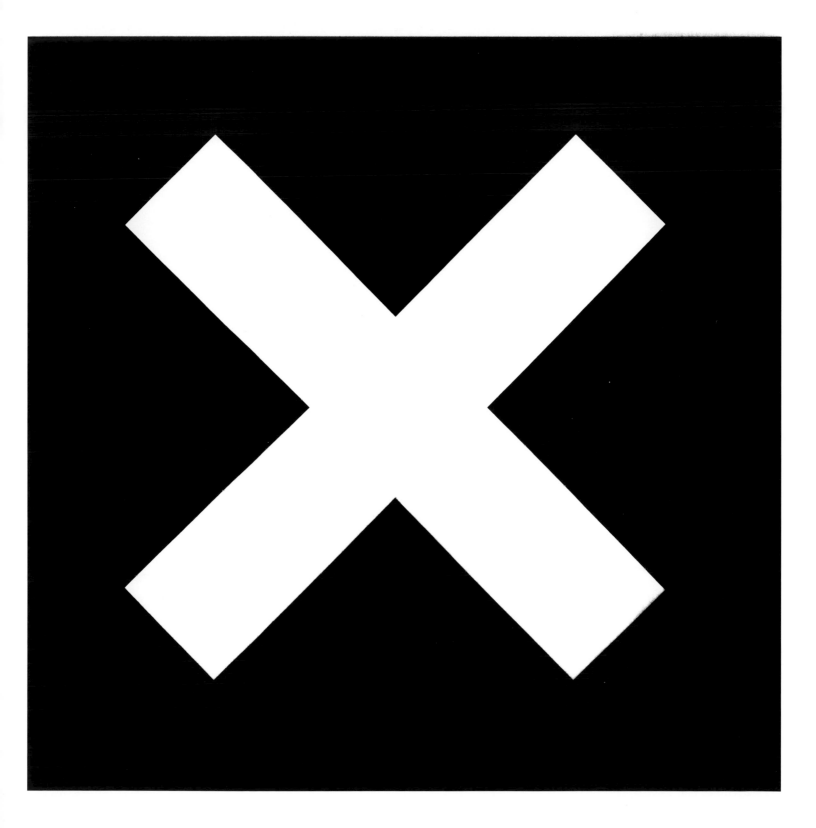

INDEX

PICTURE CREDITS

133 © 1976 Island Records. VMP © 2013 Island Def Jam Music Group. Illustration Tony Wright; 135 David Corio/Michael Ochs Archives/Getty Images; 136 © 1970 Decca, 1971 MCA; 141 © 2004 Stones Throw Records. Design Jeff Jank, photography Eric Coleman; 142 © 1998 Circa Records Ltd. Art direction & design Robert Del Naja & Tom Hingston, photography Nick Knight; 145 sjvinyl/Alamy © 1971 Reprise Records. Art direction Gary Burden, photography Tim Considine; 146 © 1991 Creation Records. Cover Designland, photography Angus Cameron; 149 © 1978 CBS Inc. Cover painting Susanna Clark; 150 © 1998 Merge Records. Art direction Chris Bilheimer & Jeff Mangum, art Brian Dewan; 153 © 2006 Drag City Inc. Design Richard Good, art Benjamin A Vierling; 154 © 1994 Geffen Records. Art direction & design Robert Fisher, photography Frank Micelotta & Jennifer Youngblood-Grohl; 157 © 2000 LaFace Records. Art direction & design Mike Rush, photography Michael Lavine; 158 © 1992 Matador Records/Big Cat Records; 161 © 1988 4AD. Art direction & design Vaughan Oliver, photography Simon Larbalestier; 162 © 2008 Go! Discs Ltd. Under exclusive license in the United States to the Island Def Jam Music Group. Design Marc Bessant; 165 WENN/Alamy; 167 © 1987 Paisley Park Records/ Warner Bros Records. Art direction Laura LiPuma, photography Jeff Katz; 168 © 2002 Interscope Records. Art direction Hutch; 171 © 2001 EMI Records. Design Stanley Donwood, art Stanley Donwood & Tchocky; 172 © 1971 Signpost Records/Regal Zonophone; 175 © 1984 Twin/Tone Records. Photography Dan Corrigan; 176 © 1971 Rolling Stones Records. Cover Andy Warhol; 179 © 1981 Anthem Records. Art direction & design Hugh Syme, photography Deborah Samuel; 183 © 1970 Flying Dutchman/BMG. Design Lou Querait, photography Charles Stewart; 184 © 2005 EMI; 187 Mick Hutson/Redferns/Getty Images; 189 © 1986 Paul Simon, Warner Bros. Art direction Jeffrey Kent Ayeroff & Jeri McManus, design Kim Champagne, photography Mark Sexton; 190 © 1967 RCA Victor. Photography David Hollander; 193 © 1997 Kill Rock Stars. Layout Neil Gust, photography Debbie Pastor; 194 © 1975 Arista Records. Design Bob Heimall, photography Robert Mapplethorpe; 197 © 1986 Rough Trade Records. Layout Caryn Gough; 198 © 1997 Dedicated. Concept Farrow Design, design Farrow Design & Spaceman; 201 © 1969 Atlantic Records; 202 © 1982 Columbia. Design Andrea Klein, photography David Kennedy; 205 Richard McCaffrey/Michael Ochs Archive/Getty Images; 207 © 2011 4AD. Design St Vincent, photography Tina Tyrell; 208 © 1977 ABC Records; 211 © 2005 Asthmatic Kitty Records. Artwork Divya Srinivasan; 212 © 2001 Rough Trade/RCA. Photography Colin Lane; 215 © 1977 Red Star Records. Artwork Timothy Jackson; 216 © 1980 Sire Records; 219 © 1976 Vertigo. Art Jim Fitzpatrick; 220 © 2006 Zomba Recordings. Design Lloyd (&Co). Photography Terry Richardson; 223 © 1993 Jive/Zomba Recordings; 224 © 2006 Touch and Go; 227 © 1996, 2014 RCA Records. Photography Keith Bardin; 228 © 1977 The Tomato Music Co. Design Milton Glaser, photography Steve Salmieri. Courtesy of Fat Possum Records; 231 © 1992 Island Records; 233 Bleddyn Butcher/REX Shutterstock; 234 © 2014 Secretly Canadian. Art direction Adam Granduciel, design & layout Daniel Murphy, photography Dusdin Condren; 237 Jordi Vidal/Redferns/Getty Images; 239 © 2015 Brainfeeder. Layout Adam Stover & Sol Washington, art "The Elixir" by Patrick Henry Johnson, photography Mike Park; 240 © 2008 Roc-A-Fella Records. Artwork J P Robinson & Kaws, photography Willy Vanderperre; 243 © 2003 V2/Third Man Recordings. Artwork The Third Man, layout Bruce Brand at Arthole, photography Pat Pantano; 244 © 2002 Nonesuch Records. Art direction & design Lawrence Azerrad, layout Jeff Smith, photography Sam Jones; 247 © 2009 Young Turks. Art direction Phil Lee & the xx.

AFTERWORD

A reminder to not be a Vinyl Elitist

I don't know why, but something about the process of getting into vinyl can make you an asshole if you're not careful. "Not me," you'll say, as you read this and stir your cream into your afternoon tea. "I'm not one of those people." Yeah, nobody is; until all of a sudden, they are.

You like these bands and not those. You like these speakers and not those. You like these turntables and not those, and so on . . .

There's nothing wrong with that—taste is the lifeblood of music for non-musicians, and for music writers it's the way we make our living. Taste rules (even more so, debating taste rules) and having a specific taste doesn't make you an asshole. The danger comes when your taste becomes more important than the music itself, and you forget that "taste" is entirely subjective.

It's important to not let what kind of turntable someone uses become more important than their stories of how they came to the records they play on it, and how those records have shaped their life. Not all of this is about you and how other people's choices line up with yours. And it's not about me either.

It's a hard line to walk, and I'm in just as much danger as anyone else. So I wanted to use this space to pen a short reminder to you (and to me) that, for those of us who don't make the music, the unifying thing here is the sacred place it has in each of our lives: the way it, in some mysterious way, creates or re-creates each of us and brings us together. The way it introduces us to ourselves, and to each other, in a way that nothing else that humans make or discover ever will. Period.

So let's stop caring so much if someone owns an all-in-one setup, or a rig that costs more than a family car. Let's stop caring so much what weight the record is, or what number out of 100 your pressing is, or indeed where that album was pressed. All of that stuff is cool, but it's not cooler than the music, and don't let anyone tell you any different.

It's OK for each of us to love the hell out of this stuff and not be an asshole about it.

Tyler Barstow
Vinyle Me, Please co-founder, 2016

ACKNOWLEDGMENTS

The publishers would like to thank:
Steve Hoped, Aiden Leacy and Jake Holloway at Love Vinyl, Lorian Reed-Drake, Giulia Hetherington, Kevin Hawkins, Trevor Davies, and Matthew Grindon for their kind assistance supplying vinyl for image purposes.

Tyler Barstow would like to thank:
The musicians who made each of these albums, and the ones who made all the albums we didn't have the space to include here. The whole point of this book is to give as much praise as we can to the albums and musicians who deserve it and there will never be enough space in any book to do that appropriately. Hopefully this attempt is less futile than it could have been. The writers, proofreaders, and project managers who took this from a weird idea to a reality in such a short time. The entire VMP team: Matt, Severan, Cameron, Emily, Hessler, Barnes, Paul, Hannah—it's an (actual) honor to work alongside you all every day on something that, I think, capital-M Matters. Mrs. Mabe for being the first person who thought my writing might one day matter. The jury is still out but I appreciate it. My parents for weathering the portion of my life I spent with them. And last, but far from least, Jennifer, who has, for some reason, believed in me and given me a sense of peace I never thought I'd find.

Andrew Winistorfer would like to thank:
The writers who worked on this book, because without you this thing with all our names in it wouldn't exist. The artists who made all the records we couldn't include here. Cameron Schaefer for making sure the Vinyl Me, Please team knew who I was when the company was new and I worked at Target. The rest of the Vinyl Me, Please team: Sev, Matt, Greens, Hessler, Barnes, Paul "Michael Jordan of Support," Hannah—see you all in the Slack. Can you believe this is our job? My parents, Carol and Wayne, for introducing me to the Doobie Brothers and for encouraging me to do this even when they couldn't hold my writing in their hands and when it mostly stunk. And last but not least Amanda, who made sure this book had Nina, and without whom my life would be meaningless.

For Abrams

Editor: Emma Jacobs
Design Manager: Liam Flanagan
Production Manager: Alex Cameron

For Cassell

Commissioning Editor: Hannah Knowles
Editor: Pollyanna Poulter
Creative Director: Jonathan Christie
Designer: Ben Brannan
Production Controller: Sarah Kulasek-Boyd

Library of Congress Control Number: 2016948799

ISBN: 978-1-4197-2597-5

Text © Vinyl Me, Please 2016
Design and Layout © Octopus Publishing
Group Ltd 2016

First published in Great Britain in 2016 by
Cassell, a division of Octopus Publishing Group
Ltd, Carmelite House, 50 Victoria Embankment,
London EC4Y 0DZ www.octopusbooks.co.uk

Printed and bound in China
10 9 8 7 6 5 4 3 2 1

Abrams Image books are available at special
discounts when purchased in quantity for
premiums and promotions as well as fundraising
or educational use. Special editions can also be
created to specification. For details, contact
specialsales@abramsbooks.com or the address below.

ABRAMS
The Art of Books

115 West 18th Street
New York, NY 10011
abramsbooks.com